CH.

1. Rob Black, Porn Drama, & ECW

How many entertainment industries exist that are more controversial than professional wrestling and pornography? With storylines that have touched on subjects from public crucifixion, necrophilia, and racism to sexism, gay marriage, and intellectual ˙ disabilities, pro wrestling is not always suitable for the entire family. Likewise, porn was a central concern during the Nixon administration and returned to the public eye again during the George W. Bush administration. Consequently, each business has sparked its fair share of mainstream disapproval.

Each, that is...

While both of these industries tend to target similar fanbases (young to middle-aged males), they are two distinct two facets of "entertainment." However, what if they were to be intermixed with one another? How would people react to wrestlers making cameos in porn productions and porn stars appearing on wrestling cards? Furthermore, who would ever dare to engage in such a financially and reputationally risky venture?

Meet Rob Zicari. As the figurehead behind the former-Extreme Associates pornography corporation and Xtreme Pro Wrestling (XPW) promotion, Zicari (better known by his alias "Rob Black") was the most controversial man in two controversial businesses: wrestling and porn.

In 2003, everything – the lawsuits, the critics, the debts, the disgruntled ex-employees, the scandals – finally caught up with him. Black and his then-wife, Janet Romano (a.k.a. "Lizzy Borden"), were indicted by the U.S. federal government for selling obscene videos across state lines.

Controversy, however, was nothing new to Rob Black. In fact, many pundits of both porn and pro wrestling have claimed that controversy is what motivates him, perhaps even what he *lives* for.

Before he became the notorious California porn figurehead who faced up to half a century in prison, Rob Black, who hails from Sicilian ancestry, grew up as a Rochester, NY native. He participated in the Golden Gloves Boxing league as a teenager and even once aspired to be a DEA agent, but none of this was meant to be; he dropped out of college in order to enter the family business of porn.

After all, his uncle Chuck ran his own porn enterprise, Zane Entertainment, dating back to 1983, while Black's father Dominic was the first person in Western New York to own adult entertainment bookstores. According to Black's September 2000 interview with RogReviews.com's Roger T. Pipe, Dominic "never had pornography around the house," but the young Black was fully aware of his father's vocation. In the late '80s, when the government was cracking down on porn's content, Dominic felt the repercussions, being arrested, Black told Pipe, about 170 times for crimes that included selling obscene materials.

None of this changed Black's decision to pursue porn. When he first met famed adult film star Tom Byron on the set of a porn movie, Black was only about 20 years old, while Byron was in his early thirties. Byron initially resented Black's "boisterous" demeanor, which he considered "kind of the opposite of [his own] personality," according to Byron's May 2000 interview with Pipe. Byron drove Black to the annual Adult Video News (AVN) awards show, but refused to accompany him in, instead handing him his business card. Black tried to contact Byron for advice when he began planning the filming of his first porn movie, but his calls weren't returned.

Black was determined to direct his own porn film with or without Byron's support. So, basically broke at the time, he used the money his father had designated as his college funds and flew into New York a crew to shoot his first movie, *Tender Loins 1*. "Basically, it was money I wasn't authorized to use," he told Pipe. "I basically stole the money to shoot the first movie."

It was during the rise of his Rochester area company, Extreme Video, that the "Rob Black" alias was born. Black told PBS *Frontline* in 2001 that his goal was "to direct movies that are just out there." He constructed Extreme Video as an alternative in an industry that he believed wasn't living up to its purpose, telling PBS:

"I sat back and I said, 'Well, you never see movies that are edgy...It's either just an all-sex movie or it's a plot about the pizza guy who delivers a pizza, and the girl doesn't have money, so she has sex with him for the pizza...Let's get a representation of life, the grittier edge.'"

Upon learning how the college money had been misused, Dominic Zicari was no happy camper, Black recalled to Pipe:

"I knew I was in trouble. He confronted me. 'You stole this, you stole that' and I was like 'Yeah, but I'm going to make all this money.' It became a shouting match. 'Fuck you,' 'No, fuck you,' and I just left."

This was 1996. Black had a vision of what he wanted to accomplish in porn and he wasn't going to achieve it while living in New York around his father's rules. So, he made a decision that may have changed the course of his life, including whether XPW would have ever been formed and whether he would have been indicted for obscenity. Black and his then-girlfriend, porn actress Tricia Devereaux, moved to California, where he stayed for about two decades. It was a year and a half before he and his dad returned to speaking terms.

There is no place on Earth that Black was meant to be more than the Golden West. He started out broke again, and once gaining porn employment, he clashed with his bosses, such as VCA Pictures' Russell "Russ" Hampshire and Elegant Angel's Patrick Collins. They gave him pushback and in some cases had screaming matches with him as to whether the violent aspects (choking, etc.) of his films were too controversial for even the porn industry.

Brad Williams, the moderator of the RAME google newsgroup, the porn equivalent of wrestling's RSPW, stated on RAME back then that "Black is going for making sex as 'dirty and disgusting' as anyone can imagine." Meanwhile, porn journalist Luke Ford described Black's films on the British TV show *Disinfo* as "the most repellent, vile, disgusting, morally troublesome work of which I'm aware." Rather than deny these claims, Black concurred with and embraced them, on *Disinfo* calling his productions "the filthiest of the filth...There's the drug dealer and we're a little above that." He later told PBS that he is one to "enjoy the challenge" and "the drama" of making "taboo" subjects "grow and thrive," while he said in the January 1998 issue of AVN that "If I can shock someone, titillate them, arouse them, make them say, 'What is this?' I'm doing my job."

CZW promoter John Zandig told me that from what he had heard, Black, bitter about not getting invited to porn conventions, used to book suites at nearby hotels and film movies there the same day to supposedly stick it to rival porn executives. On the May 13, 2020 *Rob Black Show*, Black seemingly admitted that while he had a rough exterior, he wanted to be welcomed into the porn community:

"I was that anti-establishment, but deep down inside I wanted to be accepted by the establishment. I wanted to be invited to all the cool parties and I wanted to be included in all the cool things that all the other [porn] executives...were."

This strategy seemed to work for Black. Despite straddling the line of decency, he was living the good life by late 1997, smoking three packs of cigarettes daily and driving a brand new BMW. He and then-fiancée Devereaux lived in a half-million dollar home that was "complete with diving pool, tennis courts and stables – in an 'exclusive, gated community," according to a November 22, 1997 edition of *The Guardian*.

Black's greatest achievement, though, may have been that by late 1996, he had succeeded in impressing Byron, the same person who hadn't taken him seriously a few years earlier. They found some common ground when working together at Elegant Angel, and their friendship bloomed even more in early 1998 during, as the April 1998 AVN edition worded it, "a dispute between the directors and Elegant Angel owner Patrick Collins over the directors' contracts, including salaries, revenue sharing, and ownership of titles." Collins, who had hired Black for one movie monthly at $10,000 each after Black initially rejected an offer of $5,000 each, later told Pipe that Black was "one of the worst selling directors I ever had."

Black told AVN in May 1998 that "We were walking away from six-figure incomes because we felt we were worth more on the open market." Even though contract re-negotiation attempts fizzled during a February 1998 meeting, Collins apparently had second thoughts about discharging Black and Byron. So, Black fought back like only he would, threatening to stage a literal "protest march" in front of Elegant Angel's headquarters if Collins didn't release them. Upon realizing that he'd face a two million dollar lawsuit if he didn't let Black and Byron out of their contracts, Collins surrendered. LukeFord.com reported that Black launched Extreme Associates (EA) with a $90,000 loan from Dominic.

During EA's early days, Black began dating Borden, one of his actresses. Borden explained in a March 2001 interview with Pipe that because she "came from a broken family" with an "alcoholic...abusive...stepfather" who "didn't accept me" and put her "through a lot of shit," she "was very shy and very insecure" as a youth. Working at a strip club led to her more or less falling into porn, unlike Black, who seemed destined to enter it from an early age. "I loved it because I didn't have to hide who I was," she told Pipe, adding that porn actor Luciano calling her for what was supposed to be a one-time EA scene was how she met her future-husband:

"I was worried because when I first got into the business, everyone told me never to work for Extreme, never work for Rob Black...I said, 'Fine, as long as I don't have to meet Rob Black.' Of course, I get there and the first person I meet is Rob. It turns out that he is just the sweetest guy and I can't understand why everyone hates him."

Black renamed her from "Mia Mikels" (her porn alias up until then) to "Lizzy Borden," a takeoff on 19th century accused axe murderer Lizzie Borden. In fact, there was an XPW promo photo in which she posed while holding an axe. She, along with Byron, moved in with Black. While Borden began her Extreme Associates tenure as an actress, she was appointed director within less than a year, and her EA work from mid-1999 on exclusively involved directing from the sidelines.

Early May 1998, shortly before he met Borden, was when the first inkling of involvement in the pro wrestling industry by Black developed. He was visiting relatives back East at the same time that then-ECW Tag Team Champions The Dudley Boys (Bubba Ray & D-Von) and their right-hand man, Big Dick Dudley, were in town for an autograph signing at Rochester's Ontario Video & News Store to plug a local ECW show. The store happened to be owned by Black's brother, Dominick (spelled with a "k," unlike their father's similar name), who phoned his brother and urged him to come by because Dick and Bubba wanted to meet him after viewing his porn productions. Black spent most of the day chatting with Dick and, even more so, Bubba next to a waterhole near Dominick's store. Black, had been fascinated by wrestling since childhood, and was also an ECW enthusiast. He can, in fact, be seen wearing an ECW t-shirt and cap in some of his older productions (such as *Jane Waters' The Pornographer*), while he praises ECW in the sixth scene of EA's *Free At Last* film.

The conversation in Rochester resulted in Black and his entourage being invited to attend two upcoming live events in Louisiana where they could talk business matters with ECW officials, particularly promoter Paul Heyman. In Baton Rouge on May 29, mobs of fans confronted the porn cortège for autographs. Byron was a hit not only with the audience, but also with members of ECW, several of whom teased him from the ring in between matches about how he was the most popular man in the building that night. Black's then-girlfriend Nikki Strassner also was quite an attraction among the primarily male fans; this was before Borden entered Black's life. One attendee actually touched Strassner's butt and consequently was expelled from the venue by ECW's security team. Visible on the RF Video fancam video of the event is both pornographers leaning over the guardrail and heckling Bubba and Big Dick as they made their entrance.

The next night, in New Orleans, Bubba exchanged words with Black and Byron before his match, Joel Gertner introduced Big Dick as "Tom Byron's favorite wrestler," and Sandman and Tommy Dreamer forcibly poured a Budweiser down Byron's throat, all of which is visible on the event's fancam. According to one porn media report from back then, Bubba also responded to Black's calling him a "motherfucker" by attacking the Extreme Associates owner with some shots to the crotch, and Byron, after being ridiculed by Bubba, whacked the Dudley Boy with a beer bottle several times and gave him a chairshot. However, if those things did indeed happen, they don't seem to be visible on tape.

Black and his gang's fraternization with ECW's wrestlers and employees continued after the show ended and into the following day, as they mingled off-camera with Dreamer, New Jack, Justin Credible, Francine Fournier, Shane Douglas, Danny Doring, The Blue Meanie, and Heyman. In fact, Doring can be seen wearing an Extreme Associates t-shirt at Guilty As Charged 1999.

Future-XPW wrestler and booker Douglas told me that his first encounter with Black came when he and Chris Candido were returning from a workout and Black was eating breakfast with Bubba, so they sat down and started talking to him. What stood out most to Douglas about Black was "how ridiculously he was dressed...a bright blue velvet shirt [and] weird hat."

ECW personality Lance Wright recalls that in New Orleans that weekend, the wrestlers and adult film posse entered a Bourbon Street porn store. Some female employees told them that the store was closed and they couldn't enter. Then, Dick pointed to Byron and asked if they had any idea what porn legend they were in the presence of. At that point, they recognized Byron, took photos with him, and let the group into the store.

Black continued meeting with Heyman over the next few months to discuss co-promotional possibilities. On December 26, 1998, Black, Byron, and Black's new girlfriend Borden appeared at an ECW event in Queens, NY, accompanying Sal E. Graziano and future-XPW wrestler Little Guido to the ring. Later that same night, Borden was in the ring with the Dudley family and they teased that she would show her breasts, before insulting the fans.

A week and a half later in early January, Dick and Bubba accompanied Black and Borden to the Consumer Electronic Festival (CES) show in Las Vegas and even interjected themselves on Black's behalf in a confrontation with the wife of rival director John Bowen ("John T. Bone"). A few weeks later, Black told LukeFord.com his side of the events, saying that "Out of the blue, Mrs. John Bowen starts calling me names." Hours later, Mrs. Bowen supposedly came and spit on Black as he and his crew were waiting for a taxi. Then, at the CES-sponsored dinner that same night, Mrs. Bowen confronted Black, Borden, and the two wrestlers and began yelling at them, particularly Black. Borden ended up losing her temper and called Mrs. Bowen a "fucking pig," which (according to Black) sparked Mrs. Bowen to threaten them with "a fucking bottle. Big Dick Dudley twisted it out of her hand. Then Bubba Ray Dudley told Bowen, 'If your fucking wife hits anybody with a bottle, you're going down.'" Bowen, Black says, then apologized for his wife's actions.

Despite the increasing signs of a relationship between ECW and Black, AVN president Paul Fishbein still had his doubts. Black's opinion was that AVN management "thought that because [then-AVN writer] Gene Ross and I are friends that it was just BS publicity." Not willing to accept any skepticism about the budding interpromotional association, Black thought of an idea: "Well, I did them one better. I brought one of the five-time tag team champions of the world into the AVN offices."

That's right. Black responded by bringing Bubba Ray Dudley to AVN's office on December 29, 1998, completely unannounced. Fishbein told LukeFord.com that AVN staff "were in an editorial meeting" when Byron, Black, Bubba, and an EA cameraman stormed in. The cameraman taped a wrestling-style confrontation in which, Black said in a phone conversation with Ford later that day, Bubba "got into a big pissing match with Fishbein," telling him that Extreme Associates should win some of AVN's awards. Some photographers snapped pictures of Bubba, in Black's words, "putting his hands around Paul Fishbein's neck and squeezing. Paul was visibly uncomfortable, putting his hand on Bubba Ray's hands to try to pull them off his neck." Shortly after the incident, Fishbein told Ford that he "liked Bubba and the whole thing was fine," but that, even so, it still felt a bit "weird and uncomfortable...The pissing match really was like wrestling actually because it didn't feel real at all."

Around roughly the same time, Fishbein pointed out that AVN "wrote a ton about the wrestling stuff before it happened and it has been slow developing." He insisted that he "never thought [Black] was full of shit," and emphasized that "for marketing, talking about it will not get you a nomination for Best Campaign. But if it materializes (as it looks like it will) it will be a great coup for Extreme and [Black] can market to the mainstream."

With Bubba, Dick, Dreamer, and Francine already in town, staying at Black and Borden's house to celebrate the New Year's holiday, Black ended up bringing everyone except Francine to EA's studios. The final cut of the *Whack Attack 5* production features some of this footage, including Bubba, Dick, and Dreamer (who Joey Ryan says in his Kayfabe Commentaries *YouShoot* interview is a huge porn fan) watching a sex scene be filmed. Other footage on the tape includes Lizzy hugging Bubba, ringside footage by EA's cameraman from ECW's December 1998 Queens show where the fans were chanting for Byron and Borden, and Bubba cutting a funny, vulgar promo on Black to a camera in the backseat while driving a vehicle that's street-racing Dick's car.

According to Black's ScoopsWrestling.com interview in mid-2000, during the shooting for that movie, Dreamer was filmed talking by phone with then-WCW wrestler Raven, but the clip was removed from the final cut of the movie at Dreamer's request, as he didn't want to risk WCW legalities for Heyman. The EA owner also claimed in another interview that at one point during New

Year's weekend, he himself talked with ECW star Taz on the phone for a few minutes. When asked about the day he attended the porn shoot, Dreamer said that he was invited by Dick and Bubba, that this was one of the "three or four times" he met Black and Byron, and that he was also introduced to Black's then-girlfriend, Borden.

East coast wrestling promoter Sheldon Goldberg says Dreamer told him that his *Whack Attack 5* cameo was edited to make it look like Dreamer was in the room watching the entire scene, but in reality he was only there at the beginning and end of the scene, and instead was walking around the different rooms during most of it. Dreamer told me that while he didn't sign any document authorizing the footage of him to be put out in the film, he "couldn't care less" about it being published.

In the early morning hours of New Year's Day 1999, the ECW and porn contingent were leaving West Hollywood's Rainbow Bar & Grill when a drunk man antagonized and spit at Byron, who, himself intoxicated, flicked a cigarette into the man's face. The man lunged at Byron, but Big Dick beat him into a "bloody heap" in a matter of seconds. Police were called, but the group escaped any trouble, as the stranger had initiated the confrontation. They then drove to Byron's house, where Black and Dreamer played the Madden video game "until the sun came up."

According to the February 1999 AVN issue, the second *Asswoman* film was, before the EA/ECW relationship fell apart, originally supposed to feature non-sex appearances by Bubba and Big Dick (described as "the Dudley brothers," but not individually specified), Dreamer (specifically identified), and "the owner of ECW" (only referred to as that and not mentioned by name). Per 2020 and 2021 text message conversations, Dreamer indicated that he had no comment on the reported cameo plans for *Asswoman*. Paul Heyman's lawyer, meanwhile, stated by e-mail in 2020 that Heyman was at no time involved in any negotiations to appear in the film, that the AVN article did not mention Heyman by name, and that the report must have been referring to another ECW owner or be entirely untrue.

Black told ScoopsWrestling.com that one time, Heyman spent the day with Black discussing business and stayed at his house overnight. Most of the discussions between Black and ECW transpired in February 1999. An article from that period states that during that month, Black and Heyman negotiated together for "nearly 20 hours."

Eventually, Black and Heyman reached what they thought was an agreement. Both parties agreed to advertise the other's product on their videos. An April 17 article on RAME indicated that Heyman intended to air on ECW's home videos and TV show 60 second ads for "Black's new 'Tits and Ass' line of porno action figures as well as other Extreme Associates projects." That RAME post, and also a March 3 AVN article (Rob Black Finalizes Wrestling Deal) indicated that a Tom Byron figurine would be based on his porn character and "will probably contain a toy camera and toy bed," while one of then-EA porn star Jasmin St. Claire would depict her as an ECW valet. The March 3 AVN article and two RAME posts that "'skits' [which] will be Tom Byron 'casting calls,' for porno movies" were discussed for airing on ECW TV, similar to WWE's Val Venis skits back then. In return, Black planned to use footage that EA cameramen filmed of him at ECW shows *and* footage that ECW provided him to "run trailers for the ECW product" on EA home videos, 80,000 of which were selling per month, according to Black's ScoopsWrestling.com interview.

Black also intended to use his sister porn company, Extreme Brazil, to expand ECW's product into South America. Whether ECW live events being run in Brazil was discussed is disputed, as the April 17 RAME post specifically says they weren't, but an RSPW press release mentions that possibility and, similarly, Black stated in the March 3 AVN article that "We'll also be doing live wrestling shows in Brazil. I'll be the Brazilian ECW representative."

Nonetheless, what is known for sure (as AVN, RAME, and RSPW articles, as well as Black interviews years later confirm it) is that Black was going to market ECW videos and do Internet promotion for ECW in Brazil. Black told ScoopsWrestling.com that Heyman was going to let EA "buy his masters and distribute his product in Brazil." Black elucidated about these plans on March 12 to AVN:

"I'm trying to work this Brazilian deal to distribute the tapes. Trying to hammer out the final things. The Brazilians like real stuff. They want it to be real. We're trying to put the matches together that look the most realistic - the barbed wire, the scaffolds. It's a fucking nightmare. I'm looking at a bunch of tapes of a scaffold match where the guy falls like 20 feet to the ground. It's back and forth with ECW, trying to watch these tapes, trying to decide if we're going to make a compilation of the best five extreme matches. We're going to release it; we just don't know what or when."

Goldberg wrote in a July 1999 1Wrestling.com article that running West coast ECW shows may have been considered. "Black would have assumed some sort of local promoter role, but ECW was reluctant to commit, since their TV in the market was felt to be inadequate," Goldberg wrote.

His write-up also stated that ECW considered "using some of Extreme's girls in valet-type roles." Black claimed to ScoopsWrestling.com that Heyman conceived the idea of "an Internet company" that ECW TV and home video commercials would advertise by saying "'Do you want to see Jasmin St. Claire vacuuming the carpet?' and it would show her vacuuming.' Dial up www. Whatever it was going to be'...As you go a couple of more clicks it says, 'To see explicit action and you're 18, click here'." Black said that this promotional strategy would've cost him and Heyman a combined $20,000 monthly and that he had intended to promote this product "under the censors, under [Heyman's] local people so they would never give a shit. They wouldn't know." From Heyman's perspective, the EA deal probably seemed promising in that it maybe could have improved ECW's video production, given that EA owned special cameras, lighting equipment, VCRs, and editing suites and was more financially stable than ECW's VHS-dubbing house, RF Video.

EA's Jasmin made her ECW debut on March 21, 1999 at the Living Dangerously Pay-Per-View. She, Black, Borden, and Byron flew out of California on Thursday evening to Asbury Park, NJ and attended some pre-Pay-Per-View parties on Friday night. The porn group sat in on Jasmin's Saturday morning training session with Francine, who she would be working with on-screen the following night. Going into the event, Black told Gene Ross about the plans for Jasmin's involvement:

"Jasmin's going to come out during the opening of the show. She'll be on microphone and throughout the show she'll come out with a mic talking to the people....Jasmin's the bad girl...Jasmin's scared to death that she's going to get hurt. I told her 'Nothing's going to happen.' Depending if Jasmin pisses me off between now and then I might have to tell Francine to work a little stiff. Francine'll just fucking take her out, but Jasmin's going to have to learn in three hours to get hit without it hurting."

Black, Byron, and Borden sat in the crowd for the event itself on Sunday, although they didn't appear on camera.

Shortly after Living Dangerously, however, the relationship between Black and ECW soured. Steve Karel, ECW's business manager who had previously worked for porn company Penthouse, had once tried to sell the rights of a Jasmin movie that he had filmed to Black's label. When Black told him straight up that "this movie is a hunk of shit," Karel took offense, according to Black's ScoopsWrestling.com interview, in which Black had strong words for him:

"He so desperately wanted to be in the porno business, but everything he did was just garbage. I was essentially everything Steve Karel wanted to be. I was the big pornographer. I was the one who owned the biggest company in the business. I was the one who was the player in the porno business and he wanted to be the player. And I shunned his stupid fucking movie."

Karel ignored two e-mail requests for comment about Black in 2020.

Although Goldberg claimed on 1Wrestling.com that the deal fell through because "ECW was presenting a relationship that was too one-sided for [Black's] taste," the real nail in the coffin occurred when ECW began negotiating a TV deal with TNN. Heyman cut all ties with Black and EA, refused to take his calls, and even, according to some stories, asked "Who?" when Black was mentioned.

Bubba was also affected by ECW's policy change, as he became concerned in mid-1999 that the WWE contract he was negotiating could be reneged upon if WWE found out about his appearance in *Whack Attack 5*. Black described Bubba to ScoopsWrestling.com as "a pawn in the game" because he, as opposed to Heyman, Karel, or another ECW office worker, had to be the one to phone Black and plead with him to cancel the film's publication, only to be told that it had already been released. The cameo never turned into a problem for Bubba, or for that matter, Dreamer. The former went on to be inducted into the WWE Hall Of Fame and the latter mentioned XPW on a 2005 WWE *Byte This!* webcast, and told me a year later that he "always considered XPW just another indie for guys to work. Whoop de doo."

Bubba's dream was to direct a porn scene, as he admitted in a May 2014 *Talk Is Jericho* interview:

"[Rob] was a huge wrestling fan and I was a big porn fan and he said I would love to be involved with wrestling and I said I'd love to direct some porn. [The] next week, we were doing it...[Rob] goes 'You can have any star you want - any porn star you want - you name her and I will get her for you so you can direct her' and I said 'I want Ron Jeremy.'"

In the scene, which is part of EA's movie *Fuck Pigs 1*, Bubba has two actresses make ECW references to the penis sizes of Big Dick Dudley and Dreamer, while Jeremy mentions a "Mr...P. Heyman."

Bubba kept in contact with Black while in WWE and would visit him when he was in town. Kris Kloss recalls one time Bubba was watching a blowjob scene being filmed and the camera panned in his direction. He yelled something like "Wait a minute! You can't have me on camera. I'm an employee of a Fortune 500 company. My career would be over!" Kloss also claims that Bubba once showed a tape of XPW TV to some WWE wrestlers, who supposedly enjoyed the commentary team. Kraq, meanwhile, one time told Bubba (a New Yorker) "You sound just like Rob" and Bubba responded, "No, Rob sounds just like me."

Similarly, after a WWE show in So-Cal in March 2001, Bubba introduced Godfather, Chris Jericho, Road Dogg, and Christian to Black at the Rainbow, according to a GeneRossExtreme.com report. Byron met X-Pac, who Ross wrote "was and still is a huge fan of Byron's work. As soon as he spotted Byron...across the room, X-Pac ran up to him to shake his hand and talk to him." Ross claimed that Byron "declined" Waltman's offer of "tickets to the following night's WWF show...saying he had to edit." I asked a question in Waltman's *YouShoot* (which sparked his heartiest laugh of the program) about his having "marked out" for Byron; Waltman down-played it and said "we marked out for each other actually...The first thing we said to each other was fuckin' 'Hey, everybody always tells me I look like you, and he's like 'Yeah, they say the same to me.'" According to Ross, though, that wasn't the case, as he specifically made it a point to write that "sometimes 'marking out' is not a two-way street."

Another time, "The Hardcore Homo" Angel, Black, Byron, Kevin Kleinrock, GQ Money, and Bubba were at the Rainbow and someone ordered beer, which was accidentally given to Angel, a non-drinker. An annoyed Bubba interjected something along the lines of "What do you mean, you don't drink? If I said that to The Undertaker, he would kick my ass!" Bubba asked Angel if the gay gimmick was a work and made a joke along the lines of "Well, if you're really gay, maybe you should go under the table and suck me off!" Someone said something to lighten the mood then that "broke the ice" (Angel's words) and they all laughed. Another time, Bubba made Kleinrock (another non-drinker) drink beer at fist-point.

Years later, Bubba told Blue Meanie that "'[breaking in] Jasmin St. Claire and Rob Black were my biggest ribs on the wrestling business." He used the same "biggest rib" lingo about them on *Talk Is Jericho*, where he also said "Those dirty people came into our [pro wrestling's] dirty business because of me." He also stated in RF Video's Team 3D shoot interview that "Rob Black would kill Paul Heyman in a fight." Candid ECW footage of Bubba wearing an Extreme Associates hat while sitting with Heyman made it onto WWE's 2014 Heyman DVD.

Heyman, meanwhile, had no contact with Black after their early 1999 fallout. In 2006 at a WWE show at the ECW Arena, Heyman's first time back at the building since the original ECW ran there, he referenced XPW during his promo. A show recap transcribed his words as "On a shoot, I don't care what losers and wannabes and **porno rejects** have run here. I have been dying for five years to say we are home in the ECW Arena!" Then, in a 2009 article for *The Sun* that Heyman wrote himself, he called Black a "porn impresario" who, like many other promoters he also named, had tried and failed to recapture ECW's success. Furthermore, in a 2005 Mike Mooneyham article on Hardcore Homecoming, Heyman said that Shane Douglas tried to bring back ECW with XPW and "he failed."

Speaking of Douglas, he said in his 2003 RF Video shoot interview that Black was "very similar to Paul Heyman" in that both are "very eccentric," that "they both believe their own bullshit," and that "both of them have trouble combing their hair in the morning." Douglas added that the similarities between them is "why they hate each other's guts so much." Douglas recalled in an October 8, 2019 *Franchised with Shane Douglas* podcast that Black "had a great affinity for Paul Heyman and ECW" and sometimes "likened himself to" Heyman. Additionally, Black partly used his father's money to finance his porn endeavors for years and, according to what Joey Styles and Shane Douglas have said in my presence - and other people have said it, too - Heyman used his father's money to finance ECW. Furthermore, both Black and Heyman were brash and outspoken personality-wise, had problems paying their talent at times, and found themselves involved in controversy such as lawsuits.

In 1999, Black's future in pro wrestling wasn't nearly as clear-cut as those of future-WWE mainstays Bubba and Heyman were. ECW reneging their negotiations with EA left him to decide whether he truly wanted to embark on a wrestling-related endeavor, and if so, how to go about doing so. Black explained the situation in an unidentifiable interview once: "I had been working with some guys from a local wrestling company and had been tossing about the idea of starting my own company, but was waiting to see what would happen with ECW. When Paul bitched out, I decided to go ahead full force." Who were those local wrestlers Black referred to? That's where a man who could not have been any different from Rob Black entered the picture.

2. Precursors & the development of XPW

XPW may never have existed, at least in the form that it did, without the influence of a man named Verne Langdon. Despite his admission to having "never seen any of XPW's product," Langdon (who passed away in January 2011) played a significant, albeit unintentional, role in kick-starting the careers of several people who would come to comprise the XPW league. About a third of the wrestlers who competed in matches on XPW's debut live event in July 1999 credit their initial training to Langdon's school, the "SLAM U" University of Professional Wrestling and wrestled for his Slammers Wrestling Federation (SWF). Several other people who started their careers at Slammers went on to wrestle for XPW sometime after that show, while three people (Patrick Hernandez, Danny Ramirez, and Danny Morales [Jesus Zapata/El Espirito/Felony]) who were taught the ins and outs of refereeing donned the zebra stripes in XPW.

Pro wrestling certainly wasn't Langdon's only love. As one of the pioneers of designing monster masks featured in horror movies, Langdon is still regarded as one of the most celebrated "monster-makers" (as the occupation is termed) to this day. Monster-making opened up some doors for Langdon into the fields of makeup artistry and magic, as well as writer-producer gigs and other assorted entertainment projects.

Wrestling may have been Langdon's earliest love, though. "I wrestled all my life. I always tell people I wrestled my way out of my mother's womb," Langdon explained. Even as a youngster, Langdon wrestled competitively with his cousins. Langdon himself was "taught the ropes," as he says, first by wrestler-turned-actor Tor Johnson (of Ed Wood's *Plan 9 from Outer Space* fame) and later by Moolah. "You haven't lived until The Fabulous Moolah has put the hurt on you," he joked.

Started as a ring rental facility in September 1989 in Sun Valley, CA, Slammers later became a training school and after that, a federation. "It was my great love and respect for the SPORT of wrestling that brought me to open Slammers," Langdon said. "[Moolah] was our first instructor, in addition to helping me open the gym." Moolah even mentioned her involvement with Slammers in her autobiography.

During his years as a Cauliflower Alley Club member, Langdon organized what he described as his own "private collection of memorabilia and ephemera, a compilation of gifts and contributions," consisting of wrestling-related artifacts that he inherited. One of Langdon's first steps upon opening Slammers was to use that memorabilia to establish at the facility "The Slammers World Wrestling Museum & Hall of Fame Archives," which included a wing devoted entirely to the original "Gorgeous" George Wagner. Langdon's father grappled with Wagner at the Athens Athletic Club in Oakland and Langdon remained friends with Wagner until the legend's 1963 death. The aptly named "Gorgeous George Private Collection" consisted of rare photos of Wagner, locks of his hair from a "Hair vs. Hair" match, several of his trademark robes, his wrestling boots, and other personal belongings. Langdon admits that the museum received few visitors during its operation. "Despite very favorable press (*L.A. Times*, etc.), barely a dozen people, in seven years, came to Slammers for the sole purpose of viewing the museum," Langdon said, before joking, "So much for history!"

Those students who broke in at Langdon's school and later went on to XPW had an adjustment to make, since Langdon was so drastically different from Black as both a wrestling promoter and a person. Kevin Kleinrock recalls in his July 2003 SoCalUncensored.com (SCU) interview with Steve Bryant that Langdon "liked protecting the business and wanted to kayfabe everyone from everything." Slammers trainee and XPW icon "White Trash" Johnny Webb reiterates Langdon's "old school" wrestling philosophy by citing that he would run shows every single Thursday, even if the date fell on a holiday. John Chavez (Slammers' Johnny "Angel Face" Chavez/XPW's Angel) told

Kloss on the Xtreme Memories podcast that "They were doing a video taping for something and we were students, and they actually made us leave while they were blading and made us come back. That's how old school it was."

Spending mere minutes talking with Langdon revealed a mindset just as Kleinrock, Webb and Angel describe:

"I've never been big on angles or 'storylines, entrance music or glitz. Two guys get in the ring. One's a good guy. The other is a bad guy. They wrestle. They carry the show. No managers. No frills. No pyrotechnics. No rock bands. No elephants. No tigers. No cotton candy. No peanuts. No bullshit. Just raw talent...[Slammers' product] was mostly 'passion play' wrestling, with plenty of 'cruci-fiction!' Our good guys usually won over our bad guys. I rarely honored injustice, but when I did, it was for great dramatic effect, with eventual retribution not far behind."

SWF action occasionally varied slightly from traditional wrestling, as they showcased "Steel Chair," "I Quit," "Dog Collar Chain," "Falls Count Anywhere," and "Stretcher" matches. Even then, though, Langdon aimed to keep the wrestling aspect as the focus, and points out that when SWF wrestlers did "go hardcore," they were "choir boys" compared to what he was told the wrestlers of XPW and other organizations did in years since. In fact, as time went on and over 10 of his former students joined XPW, Langdon was surprised at how many of the wrestlers among them did for Black's company stunts more dangerous than the routines that some of them had complained about doing at Slammers a short time before.

As an example of his view on the "hardcore wrestling" style, Langdon recounted how Tim "Damien Steele" Fisher asked him on a couple occasions for permission to "juice" (bleed) in his matches. Langdon turned down each request. "It made no sense in the brief course of Tim's matches in question, and I felt that if blood became a common occurrence in SWF matches, then it would lose its meaning," he explained. "Tim gave up on the blood thing pretty quickly because he got my drift." Langdon tried to ensure that when blood did show itself in an SWF ring, "it meant something, and was very disturbing - or rewarding, depending on who got busted open - to the fans."

Langdon said that certain Slammers trainees left the school because they couldn't handle the arduous instruction or became disillusioned with the sport, while some were asked to leave due to not making the necessary progress. Angel agreed on Xtreme Memories, saying that "Everybody that I would join with would either quit or couldn't hang," and Messiah said the same thing in his Smart Mark Video (SMV) shoot interview. Carlos Torres (XPW's Carlito Montana) said that most of the students who got kicked out didn't belong. Langdon says that other students who did "achieve a certain point in their training" (which was determined by him and his fellow trainers) moved on to seasoning themselves in front of fans at live SWF shows. The SWF's first show took place on October 6, 1991, but Langdon doesn't take credit for it. "As the boys learned, they wanted to actually do," Langdon explained, "so they decided they wanted an in-house 'federation.' They thought up the 'SWF,' not me."

Langdon's training strategy was based not only around teaching maneuvers and holds, but also instilling in his trainees certain life-long values. "It's in my blood to be professional and do things to the best of your ability, so that's what I tried to ingrain in them. A few actually got it," he said, citing Torres and Chavez (among others) as examples. "Unfortunately, some others just didn't," he added. Langdon emphasized that "We never promised any student he would 'see the world' and 'earn millions of dollars in wrestling,' as some schools and teachers do," just because they paid their tuition. In fact, in an interview a month after Langdon died, Terry Funk remembered it as Langdon having "let the guys go in there for nothing and stay in there for nothing" because "he was concerned about having wrestlers in there and not how much they paid him."

One of those wrestlers was Darren McMillan. He created the "Wrestle Talk" audio show in 1989 and hosted it on California cable stations every Saturday night until 1994. Ironically, some 10 years later, when he was a member of the XPW roster, McMillan (along with other XPW personalities) appeared as a guest on that very same program to advertise the then-growing XPW product. McMillan used the alias "Dynamite D" on the show, even before he became a wrestler. "An article about him ran in the local (Tujunga) newspaper," Langdon explained of his first contact with McMillan. "I called Darren at the [Wrestle Talk] station, told him about Slammers, he came over, I got him in the ring, and he was hooked." Langdon used McMillan to promote the school in TV news stories and even arranged for some guest trainers (including friends Moolah, Funk, and Sam Houston) to offer McMillan pointers during Slammers ring workouts.

In 1990, about a year after McMillan started at Slammers, Torres also came along. Although McMillan was responsible for most of Torres' technical instruction, Torres stresses "Verne's the one that taught me the philosophy. If you don't have the philosophy, you don't have shit." Torres made his wrestling debut for the SWF as the masked "Hombre de Oro" in late 1992. The mask, he says, "could be a big pain in the ass," but he eventually got used to donning it.

Torres found out about Slammers from Oscar Cecena (XPW's Pancho Killa) and Patrick Hernandez during a 1990 meeting in Target's magazine aisle. Cecena started training in 1990 and was given the "Samoan Kid" persona by Langdon for his SWF matches. Although he only lasted in Black's promotion for a few months, Langdon doesn't short-change Cecena, calling him "a really good natural heavyweight wrestler" and "one of the best 'rope-runners' I've ever seen. I had him teach running the ropes to all our other students."

McMillan and Torres both became Slammers trainers and spawned several future-XPW performers. Webb recalled in an April 2008 Rubber Guard Radio interview that at Slammers, "there were almost kind of like cliques. There were guys that were being trained just by Dynamite D and guys that were being mostly trained by Carlito Montana. There just always seemed to be some sort of a wall there." McMillan explained the distribution of training between himself and Torres:

"Carlos' training consisted of being my T.A. in the SLAM U lessons I was teaching. He would help me teach the student what a move looked like [and] how to execute it properly by taking lots of bumps and [work] with the student so I could watch the move executed and correct any mistakes...He was the one I was passing the torch to, in order to continue the expected level of excellence in training. He had the fire that was slowly (and at times, more quickly) burning out from me. Verne saw this and eventually pulled me out of training and put Carlos in full-time."

Homeless Jimmy, McMillan's real-life cousin, was among those who joined Slammers. "My uncle called me and told me my cousin was back in town and was a big wrestling fan," McMillan said. "He came to the very next Slammers event and signed up on the spot." Jimmy's willingness to perform risky stunts was evident immediately. "I knew he was dedicated and would do anything you asked him to do," McMillan explained. "I think he took a chair shot the first day of class." Jimmy started training under McMillan and Jeff Lindberg in early 1995 and debuted in the SWF as Jimmy Jaimes in December 1995. While the Homeless Jimmy character was notorious for his disheveled appearance, SWF-era Jimmy was clean cut and had short hair.

The "Homeless Jimmy" gimmick was partly conceived by Webb, who became interested in wrestling through his fandom of martial arts. Webb's instruction began in 1995 under McMillan's guidance and he debuted a year later for the SWF as "Spider" Pete Malloy. McMillan also handled most of the training of Steele (SWF's Buddy "The Body" West) and Jesse "Tyrone 'Tiny' Little" Balin, the latter of whom went on to portray XPW's short-lived "Cybil" character.

In early 1996, around roughly the same time as Steele and Balin started, future-XPW mainstay Billy Welch (The Messiah) came to Slammers. Torres, his trainer, saw "a lot of natural athletic ability" and therefore potential in Messiah, so although he took him under his wing, he was "very tough on him," compared to other students. Messiah said on a March 2020 "Shooting The Sh*t UNCENSORED!" podcast that the trainers and his fellow trainees "started calling me 'Car Crash Billy' because I looked like I went through a car crash when" they would "throw" his "166 pounds soaking wet" self "around the ring."

Messiah made his SWF debut on Thanksgiving Day 1996 at Bakersfield's Strongbow Stadium against Felony (the SWF's "El Espirito") as "Iron" Mike Ehrhardt, the storyline younger brother of more experienced Slammers wrestler Mark Ehrhardt. The nickname "Iron Mike" was bestowed upon Messiah by Langdon in honor of veteran grappler "Iron" Mike Sharpe Sr., who built Slammers' ring. Langdon emphatically disavowed claims he said Messiah made in interviews that the "Iron" Mike name came from a drunken fan who attended Slammers shows and that it was a gay gimmick. In December 1997, Messiah was filmed putting Langdon in a half nelson for the TV show *Jeopardy*, which aired in February 1998.

One of the XPW non-wrestlers who had a stay in Slammers was Kevin Kleinrock. He was the student body treasurer of his high school, and conceived the idea of holding an SWF fundraiser there. Kleinrock told SCU's Bryant:

"[The show] wasn't really a success...but we did it and I got my first check because I got like 10% of the gate. So, it was my first money in pro wrestling and it was like five bucks. I framed it and still haven't cashed it to this day…[After the fundraiser show], I started doing everything I could for Slammers. I was writing results for all the national magazines. I was ring announcing. I was timekeeping...We'd go to the meetings before the show and I'd be there to go over the ring cards."

While Kleinrock left Slammers to begin his college education at UCLA, other wrestlers departed for more personal reasons. A few of the Slammers students began grumbling among themselves about whether they had a future in wrestling if they were to remain at Slammers.

McMillan, meanwhile, inquired to Langdon three weeks before a Thanksgiving 1996 show about taking the day off to spend it with family and, according to a July 27, 2000 *L.A. New Times* article by Luke Y. Thompson, "was granted it, but was told that he wouldn't be working for Langdon again afterward."

McMillan told me he requested it "off only after hearing that" another wrestler "had requested and gotten the day off."

In early 1997, after he had left Slammers, McMillan concocted a plan based on WCW's popular nWo (New World Order). McMillan attempted to create his own spinoff called the "dWo" ("Dynamite Wrestling Organization"). "My goal was to get all the workers [Verne] had pushed out of the SWF back into the company," McMillan told me. "I wanted to get 'real' life situations with heat so that we could have exciting matches and build up the fed." McMillan was hoping that Langdon would see the idea's potential and create in the SWF a dWo storyline that incorporated the Slammers trainees who had left. Torres' account is that McMillan "was hoping we would all just jump boat" to a new organization he would spearhead.

Langdon found out through a game of "Telephone" news of the plan, which was intended to be kept a secret, via two of his wrestlers. McMillan told me that he had developed an inkling that Langdon knew ahead of time - "I wondered whether or not to still do it." Langdon didn't do anything to try to stop the situation from playing out, instead allowing them to, in his words, "have their fun."

At intermission of a June 1997 SWF show at Kleinrock's high school, McMillan and then his former-Slammers buddies stormed the ring, without prior permission. McMillan cut a "shoot" promo about Langdon and Slammers, encountered Langdon face-to-face in the ring, and proclaimed himself the leader of the dWo, even removing his t-shirt to reveal one of his custom-printed dWo t-shirts. Those who participated in McMillan's in-ring stunt included, but weren't limited to, Webb, Jimmy, Felony, and Steele, all of whom had already left Slammers. Kleinrock, Hernandez, and Ramirez (who reffed in the SWF as "Juaquim 'Jackie' Columbo") watched the incident from the crowd, but didn't enter the ring. "They all knew and all were wearing the dWo t-shirts," remembered McMillan. Kleinrock remarked to Bryant that because McMillan's promo was well received by the crowd, "everyone left the building that night thinking, 'Alright, maybe Verne will think it was a cool idea and want to do something with it.'" However, that isn't what happened. Steele says McMillan thought Langdon would "see it as a storyline and Verne took it as a personal attack" instead.

Hours after the show ended, Langdon put his own plan into action, calling Balin and telling him, McMillan, and the rest of the ring crew to not even bother setting the ring back up at McMillan's storage unit. Langdon said instead to unload it at another nearby storage facility because he was closing Slammers. He also had the Slammers web site (Slammers.com) and phone number temporarily disabled. Kleinrock says that the crew was taken aback by Landon's response, telling Bryant, "That was totally not what anyone expected or wanted him to do." Langdon successfully tricked McMillan and others into thinking that he was folding Slammers because of the incident.

As it turned out, Slammers didn't fold. Langdon stressed that contrary to others' claims, the June 26, 2000 edition of *TIME Magazine*, as well as CNN, Fox World Sports, E! TV, and Warner Bros. TV Productions coverage around the same time, showed that Slammers existed after the dWo stunt, and it also ran more shows. As a matter of fact, several new trainees joined Slammers at a new nearby location soon thereafter, among them Torres students Gabe Ramos (Slammers' Gabriel Valentino/XPW's Juantastico) and Chavez. Messiah, who didn't participate in McMillan's stunt, continued his training with Torres until 1998 before mutually parting ways from Slammers for personal reasons. However, Langdon got out of the wrestling business in 2000, so the only future-XPW wrestlers to complete their training and formally graduate were McMillan, Torres, and Cecena.

McMillan's name was on the lease for the Slammers facility, and now that Langdon had given it up, the former-SWF crew had their own ring. Kleinrock told Bryant that McMillan "wasn't going to let the opportunity pass him by to get back involved." So, Kleinrock and McMillan sought out Hernandez, who had learned refereeing from mainly Danny Ramirez and had reffed on some SWF events after starting as a cameraman. Together, the three launched Southern California Championship Wrestling (SCCW), which as Kleinrock told Bryant, showcased "just your basic rinky dink indy shows. They'd have from ten people to a hundred people at them. That was life with SCCW."

Some people who broke in at Slammers joined the roster of the upstart promotion, including Cecena, The Creeper/Skullcrusher (Homeless Jimmy), Nick Beat (Buddy West/Damien Steele), and "Sheriff"/"Uncle" Jess Hanson (Cybil). Jimmy brought a skull to the ring on a stick for his Skullcrusher persona, which Webb described on a Rubber Guard Radio episode as a character out of the film *Highlander*. Several other future-XPW talents who hadn't trained at Slammers also became members of SCCW, including Phenomenal Phil, Byron McKinney (SCCW's Ken Masters, Byron Walker, and Tech IX/XPW's Kristian Blood), Shooting Star, and "Krusher" Gary Key (TOOL in XPW). It was in SCCW that SWF wrestler Pete Malloy became Johnny Webb, while non-wrestling roles included Kleinrock as the promotion's storyline commissioner and future-XPW commentator Kris Kloss as the ring announcer. Hernandez refereed and McMillan wrestled for SCCW, in addition to being two of the promoters. SCCW also used local talent like Ron "American Wild Child" Rivera and even a young Super Dragon. The Insane Clown Posse (ICP) even attended one SCCW show, sans makeup.

SCCW's biggest show ever, entitled "SlamFest," came on May 28, 1998 and included a tag team main event involving Yokozuna and The Honky Tonk Man. The show fulfilled then-UCLA sophomore Kleinrock's obligation to host for his fraternity a fundraiser, which in this case raised money for the Make-A-Wish Foundation.

Several wrestlers who competed for SCCW also simultaneously worked for another local organization, the Impact Wrestling Federation (IWF). SCCW wrestlers Gary Key (an IWF co-owner), Shooting Star, Webb, Hanson, Cecena, Phil, and McKinney took IWF bookings. Webb says he enjoyed wrestling for the IWF, but emphasizes that he wasn't there long. One of his favorite IWF experiences was meeting Christopher Daniels, who himself wrestled about five matches for the IWF between March and June 1998. In 2006, Daniels praised Key as being very athletic for his size and told me that he particularly enjoyed the match he had against Hanson in Simi Valley on June 6.

SCCW and IWF weren't destined to find long-term success, however, and they both stopped running shows around late 1998 and early 1999. As a result, for the last six months or so until XPW opened up, several wrestlers who would go on to be in XPW, such as Skullcrusher, Webb, McKinney, Cecena, Nick Beat, Jess Hanson, Phil, and a few others, made the late Doc Marlee's United Independent Wrestling Alliance (UIWA) their home promotion. UIWA had local TV, featuring McMillan on commentary. It was also where B-Boy and Samoa Joe first started making waves. Joe's in-ring debut (which he talks about in his ROH "Straight Shootin" interview) was against the future Cybil. After the XPW-destined wrestlers left for Black's new endeavor, UIWA brought in upstarts like The Prototype (John Cena), who himself could be seen sometimes passing out UPW flyers at XPW shows a few years later.

It was in the IWF and UIWA that Kaos and Supreme met some of their future-XPW comrades. They broke into wrestling in the fall of 1994 when Supreme started training in a warehouse near Coldwater Canyon in Van Nuys, "I followed him," Kaos explains. "It was more so, I wanted to hang out with my crazy, cool uncle."

Who trained Kaos and Supreme has been disputed. When asked to set the record straight, Kaos says that So-Cal indie wrestler Crayz-1 taught himself and Supreme how to bump and build a match. Other than that, Kaos says, "I never had a trainer to go to or someone to let me know if I was doing something right or wrong. Supreme and I trained ourselves by watching a lot of All Japan tapes and taking that to the ring for trial and error."

While training, Kaos used the alias "The Rawhide Kid" for practice matches which didn't take place in front of a live crowd. "It was more of a rib Supreme and Crayz were playing on me," Kaos explains. He and Supreme trained together for about a year before making their debuts one-on-one together on July 7, 1995 in Colton in front of about 50 fans. Supreme won the match with a Moonsault Headbutt, the same move he used to defeat Kaos in the first round of the 2000 XPW death match tournament almost five years later. "[It was a] basic match. I remember being nervous as hell," Kaos reminisces.

The uncle-nephew duo continued to wrestle in various So-Cal promotions, mainly as a tag team called "Supreme Kaos."

They first started turning heads with their feud against a team known as Da Naybahoodz (Crayz-1 & Byron "Tech IX"/"Kristian Blood" McKinney), who they wrestled, Kaos says, about 50 times, between tag and singles action. The feud took off in GSWA with a tag team title win by Supreme Kaos in April 1996. It later continued in Alex Knight and Ed Arhen's American Independent Wrestling Alliance (AIWA), Johnny Legend's Incredibly Strange Wrestling (ISW), ref Dan Farren's Cal International Wrestling (CIW), and the UIWA, in several of which the teams also traded tag team titles. Kaos attributes some credit to his later success in XPW to AIWA's Arhens, saying "Ed gave me a lot of good information which helped me big time in creating the 'Rock Superstar' gimmick."

One particular ISW show where Supreme Kaos wrestled Da Naybahoodz took place on June 27, 1997 in Hollywood and featured three special guests in attendance - then-WCW wrestler Chris Jericho (who won the Cruiserweight title the next night), mainstream actor Chris Farley, and Sylvester Stallone's son Sage. Sage managed Da Nayabahoodz for their match. After the match, Jericho came up to Blood (who passed away in 2008) and told him that while the match was good, they could make improvements, as even though the fans were popping for headlocks, the wrestlers were doing crazy dives. Meanwhile, Farley (who was visibly drunk and on drugs) used the walls to balance himself as he stumbled up to Blood. He remarked how amazing Blood's Triple-Jump Moonsault was and rambled dejectedly about how he wished he could do something like that, but he was just a fat old man. Blood thought Farley was being too hard on himself and unsuccessfully tried to cheer him up, and Farley clumsily staggered back to his hotel. That night, the two teams took pictures of themselves with Farley and pictures of Farley with porn stars who were hanging out at the show, but the camera got destroyed and the pictures were lost. Farley died two months later.

Of the IWF, Kaos reminisces, "I always liked Impact, but I don't think they, IWF brass, really liked [Supreme and I]." They never joined SCCW, though. "I wanted to [be in SCCW], but the brass there had no interest in Supreme Kaos" who he thinks were "still, to a certain extent, outcast."

One of the methods SCCW used to attract new fans to its shows was to pass out flyers at WWE events. One night, WWE was running the Arrowhead Pond and, as Kleinrock told SCU, "we handed the flyer to someone through a car window and you think nothing of it. It turns out the guy was Rob Black."

A few days later, McMillan got a voicemail on his work phone from Black saying that he wanted to talk to SCCW management about a wrestling-related endeavor. McMillan called Black back and set up a meeting at TGI Fridays in Woodland Hills. Kleinrock and Hernandez came with McMillan, while Black bought along porn colleagues Gene Ross and Tom Byron.

Hernandez already had some knowledge of the porn industry and knew who Black was before he ever contacted SCCW. However, the porn business was new to McMillan and Kleinrock. the latter of whom told Bryant, "The night before we go to meet them I go on the internet, and I'm looking up their names and find this bio on Tom Byron that says 'Tom Byron is perhaps the biggest male porn star ever behind John Holmes and Ron Jeremy.'"

The night, the six men sat outside on the restaurant patio discussing what they could do together in wrestling. "I liked Rob right from the start," McMillan said. "He was a little different than most, but I expected that from a pornographer." Black recalled on his May 6, 2020 podcast that "They had books printed up - things for me to look at - of how 'successful' they were in their first show [on] a tennis court." Kleinrock has since said that "Thankfully, Rob never saw an SCCW show because if he had seen an SCCW show...he would have run in the opposite direction from us" ("Straight Outta The Bodega" podcast in May 2020) upon having "seen how rinky dink we were, even though we knew what we were capable of if we had money behind us." (Bryant SCU interview).

After more meetings with Black and his crew at various restaurants, the SCCW representatives were invited to the Extreme Associates Van Nuys office. McMillan recalled:

"It was a fun time getting to see behind the scenes in the adult industry. [Rob] gave us a tour of the offices after the first meeting and then loaded up a box full of porn for each of us. He said it was study material so we get to know who everybody was."

Black flew in Kleinrock's East coast friend Sheldon Goldberg to consult with about what was needed to start a wrestling company. Goldberg, who stayed in California for five days, laughs when he recalls the first time he met Black, saying that suddenly a limousine pulled up to the simple, elaborated "Chilli's" restaurant and out walked Black's porn entourage. "It was like a Rob Black version of The Polo Lounge," Goldberg jokes.

There were at least two other meetings involving Goldberg at EA's office. Goldberg recalls how Black mailed him a box of pornos and when he played the first tape, he immediately saw a blowjob scene take place on the same couch in front of Black's desk that he had sat on during a meeting at the office. "It made me wonder what else was on that couch with me," he jokes.

Goldberg noticed two things about Black during their meetings. The first thing was that Black was clueless about the science of professional wrestling, but he was *not* clueless about what it'd take to start a wrestling organization. He already was a step ahead of most upstart wrestling promoters in that he had video distribution, lighting equipment, editing suites, cameras, and links to semi-mainstream media. Goldberg also realized that Black was obsessed with ECW, and even more so, Heyman, saying "If he couldn't bring ECW to the West coast, he was going to create his own version of it for the West coast."

Goldberg gave Black two main points of advice, as a result - 1. Don't attach his name to the company until it developed a solid audience that would be willing to look past it being owned by a pornographer, and 2. Get people experienced in pro wrestling to assist in its operation, rather than simply relying on his porn colleagues. For the most part, Black ignored both pieces of advice. When the initial press release announcing the formation of XPW went out to the world via RSPW on June 4, 1999, a whole paragraph was devoted to Black's porn background. Regarding Goldberg's other advice, Black did use Big Dick Dudley in booking some early XPW shows, as well as Shane Douglas later on, but for the most part, the promotion was run right out of the Extreme Associates office.

McMillan recalled how the "XPW" name was conceived:

"We were coming up with a name and I said 'How about Extreme Associates Wrestling?' Rob said, 'No, ECW will sue us for sure.' Sheldon said, 'What about X, just "X" Wrestling?' I must have written down 10 things in the next two minutes [that] 'X' could stand for - 'Xciting,' 'Xcellent,' 'Xtreme,' 'Wrestling to the power of "X",' 'X marks the spot.'"

They later settled on "Xtreme Pro Wrestling" (XPW).

Before Goldberg flew back East, he invited Black to call him for any other suggestions, and they spoke once or twice again. "I didn't see him as an evil guy at all. I just think he had a blind spot when it came to [wrestling] and he didn't have enough knowledge to ascertain what was good and what wasn't." Goldberg remained in more frequent contact with Kleinrock throughout XPW's existence, saying "Kevin would call me from time to time to ask for phone numbers or to get advice."

McMillan, Kleinrock, and Hernandez continued to meet with Black and his porn staff after Goldberg left California, as the plans to create XPW developed. McMillan first met Black's then-girlfriend, Borden (real name: Janet), at a BBQ at Black's house, and he told the story best from that point on:

"She was dressed way down - sweats, baggy sweatshirt, no shoes. She was making some food and Rob was firing up the grill. He said, 'That's Janet. She lets me fuck her in the ass and she eats my cum. I guess I'll keep her around awhile.' Just the person I needed preparing my food. I wasn't hungry anyway. I was fascinated by the lifestyle they all had. Nice big house in a ritzy, gated community. Nice cars, wads of cash, and lots of hot chicks. And I thought the wrestling lifestyle was cool--at that time, indie wrestling lifestyle had nothin' on porno lifestyle."

Black also invited McMillan and Hernandez to a party at the house of porn actor Van Damage and actress Tiffany Mynx, during which the EA crew was filming a scene of the *Asswoman In Wonderland* movie. There, they met some porn hands, including future-XPW personalities Jessica and Bobby Darlin (XPW's Luis Cypher). "Bobby was a huge wrestling fan and was wearing a Stone Cold t-shirt. We all got along well," McMillan recalled. "If you see the video, you may catch a peek at me and Pat standing around while Rob says the word 'Fuck!' about 20 times."

During the course of these various meetings throughout late 1998 to mid 1999, Black (in his own words on his May 6, 2020 podcast) "inherited Kevin Kleinrock, Dynamite D, and Patrick Hernandez, along with an old, beat-up ring, and a bunch of rag-tag wrestlers" that comprised SCCW. "When I created XPW, I basically bought a company." In fact, the future-Kristian Blood recalled being asked by Hernandez several months before XPW's first show if he would main event an SCCW show with a major financial backer. That backer, as history went, turned out to be Black.

Blood was one of those people who *was* inherited by Black, but Kloss emphasized on many Xtreme Memories episodes that many of the wrestlers who had a chance to be acquired from SCCW and UIWA did *not* get bequeathed because Black didn't see value in them for various reasons. Kloss told GQ Money that Black quickly "figured out who he wanted and who he didn't based on everyone just shooting the shit, conversation throughout" and who of those people did and didn't act like "marks" around the porn office, and he made similar comments on the Hernandez, Phenomenal Phil, and other Xtreme Memories episodes. Others were weeded out by not impressing during an in-ring tryout. Kaos, Supreme, and Jimmy especially *stood out* at the tryout for being willing to go through a table.

Black was serious about blending his main priority, porn, with his subsidiary hobby, pro wrestling. He even told Luke Y. Thompson of *The LA New Times* in 2000, "I run my adult company like pro wrestling, so an actual wrestling company is a natural step." So, by cherry-picking his ideal crew and accentuating what he considered to be their positive qualities, Black created Extreme Associates' sister company, XPW.

3. The early days of XPW

Extreme Associates heavily promoted the debut show of XPW via a "media blitz" (in AVN's words), featuring ads in newspapers, as well as - starting on July 18 - commercials on WWE RAW, Sunday Night HeAT, and WCW Nitro, among other places. Webb, whose birthday was the same day as the debut show, remembers that XPW spared no expense in advertising its first show, running TV ads, flyering nearby towns, and making a beautiful program. The July 19, 1999 *Wrestling Observer* newsletter also promoted the debut, with Dave Meltzer writing "Xtreme Pro Wrestling is a new group notable if only because it will have several porn stars." July 10 saw an appearance by Black, Byron, Ashlyn Gere (who appeared in the debut show's bikini contest), Jasmin, Borden, Myst, and Webb on Ed Powers' *Bedtime Stories* radio show on 97.1 KLSX "The FM Talk Station." On July 28, Black, Borden, Myst, and Byron made an appearance on another KLSX show, *Conway & Steckler*.

XPW's debut show took place on July 31, 1999 at the Reseda Country Club, which was once a major rock and roll venue that was featured in the "Boogie Knights" movie, and the first show got TV coverage on Los Angeles' Channel 7. Kristian Blood remembered the first show as having a lot of tension backstage, with Black "nervous," Kleinrock yelling on the headset, and Phenomenal Phil trying moves he wasn't capable of. McMillan recalled the backstage atmosphere as "energetic and numbing at the same time." Ref Ramirez said there was a lot of "chaos," "screaming," and "talking shit" backstage.

Phil remembered on facebook on the 20th anniversary of the debut show that "All the boys backstage were drunk, including Missy Hyatt who kind of appeared out of nowhere. Rob ended up banning alcohol from the locker room after that." Hyatt did not appear in front of the crowd that night, although she appeared in the company months later, and word has it that alcohol too ended up finding its way back into the locker room on some occasions.

Other people have also echoed Phil's sentiments that not everyone behaved themselves at that first show. For instance, the host of a Vegas Badboyz Podcast with Kleinrock on August 9, 2019 recalled that one of his "buddies' girlfriends went to the women's restroom...and she comes back and she goes 'Well, there are about four porn chicks in there and they were doing coke right out in the open."

Additionally, Steele recalls that he invited UPW promoter Rick Bassman and the UPW brass at the show as guests. There had been a "bidding war" (Steele's words) between XPW and UPW when XPW started. Rick and his crew, Steele says, came backstage and "were asked to find seats" in the crowd. Steele thinks they ultimately sat in the balcony, and says they acted unprofessionally and critiqued the whole show. Steele was mad at Bassman for how they conducted themselves there, so he stayed with XPW and didn't go to UPW till about a year later.

Big Dick made his first XPW appearance at that debut show. He gave the other wrestlers feedback after their matches. Phil recalls on facebook that Big Dick "had some kind of weird co-management deal with Rob." Big Dick himself seemed to echo these sentiments in his Wrestling Universe shoot interview before he passed, repeatedly referring to XPW as "my company." It may have been part storyline, as at the time he was feuding with Black on XPW TV and live shows over control of the company, but there was also at least a sentiment of truth to the wording he used in his shoot interview. Dick wrestled Steele in what Steele admitted was a "lackluster performance" that featured a table refusing to break, but Steele nonetheless had a blast that first night.

Tito Ortiz, then a UFC rookie fighter, but not nearly as big of a name as he would later become, was supposed to do a squash match on XPW's first show. However, AVN reported that he cracked a rib the previous night against Frank Shamrock, although another story says he was injured in a training session. Either way, Ortiz's name was on the booking sheet for the debut show, which Kleinrock posted on facebook in the 2010s. Ortiz used to work as a clerk at *Spanky's*, an adult bookstore in Orange County. *Spanky's* sponsored him in unsanctioned MMA fights, and Black and Byron got to know him at some of these fights. Ortiz was paid by Black a few thousand dollars to put on an Extreme Associates 3:16 "I Just F*cked Your Ass" t-shirt on camera after beating Jerry Bohlander at UFC 18 on January 8, 1999 as a marketing ploy for Extreme Associates. Ortiz wrote about the shirt on pages 86 and 87 of his autobiography. Black described Tito's proposed role in a June 30, 1999 interview with Gene Ross:

"He'll be the UFC fighter in the group...Tito will be the Goldberg/Taz character - the quicker you submit, the less you suffer."

Kleinrock also hyped Tito up in a July 28, 1999 press release, saying, "Tito's skill and charisma make him one of the hottest free agents today." Ortiz was rescheduled for the August 27 XPW show, according to an XPW press release, although he did not appear on that show either. That event instead featured future-UFC legend Justin McCully vs. Mike "Lee" Young Gun in a shoot-style contest. XPW hyped the show in press releases as "the US debut of Antonio Inoki's Universal Fighting-arts Organization," since Inoki's promotion (his answer to UFC) had only run in Japan up until that point. This McCulley vs. Young Gun match, though, was the extent of the UFO-XPW cross-promotion that was realized. Only a single armbar takedown clip from the match ever surfaced in an XPW TV music video. Kleinrock said on twitter 15 years later that the match was put on the card as a favor to Simon Inoki, who was running UFO's U.S. operations.

McCulley wasn't the only oddball name who made one appearance in XPW; so did Christopher Daniels. One person who

Daniels became friendly with outside of the ring in XPW and especially later in UPW was Steele. Daniels recalled in a 2006 conversation that while they were in UPW together, he and his wife became good friends with Steele and his wife. Daniels remembers that Steele was very careful about his diet and was very devoted to exercise. Daniels worked out at the ring in XPW's offices a few times in the early days of the company at the invitation of then-Asylum trainer Steele. Daniels told me in 2006, "Kevin [Kleinrock] always wanted to do something with me and had a lot of ideas for my character" and that while Rob Black was a "nice guy" the one time he worked for XPW, Black didn't seem as enthusiastic about him as Kleinrock did.

Around that time, Daniels was working for Northern California's All Pro Wrestling (APW), which XPW established an informal relationship with. Black explained on a May 6, 2020 *Rob Black Show* that he "took the front office and/or front office friends...10 of us, 15 of us" of XPW on a "field trip" to see *Beyond The Mat* in theaters, even paying for the theater tickets. That movie is how some people in XPW management first found out about APW. Subsequently, in late 1999 and early 2000, XPW brought in some APW wrestlers, like Donovan Morgan, Mike Modest, and Tony Jones. According to Lazie, there was some talk of more talent exchanges between the two groups. Webb recalled on Rubber Guard Radio in April 2008 that bringing in the APW guys was "the first bit of effort made on our part to be more than just garbage wrestling...We were definitely trying to send that message that we weren't just a bunch of guys rolling around in thumbtacks. Not all of us."

Morgan even had a short-lived job as a trainer at the XPW Asylum Training School. He quit the gig after finding out about, and depending on who you believe, possibly walking in on, his office desk being used for a porn scene. Modest said in April 2020, "Donovan didn't quit immediately [after that incident]. He talked to me and told me it didn't feel right. He said he felt like he was working for the devil."

Lazie says that Modest and Morgan had big egos and thought they should have their own locker room. Modest denied this in April 2020, saying he was friends with a lot of the XPW wrestlers, got along with almost everyone well, and didn't want his own locker room. As time went on, XPW obtained other talents from APW, notably Steve Rizzono and Pogo The Clown (APW's Joe Applebaumer). AVN even mentioned Rizzono (misspelling his name as "Rosano") in an article on June 30, 1999 (a month before XPW's first show) as having been someone who XPW planned to use. Rizzono says that when he did join, Borden would frequently ask him to move from Nor-Cal to LA.

There was one notable incident involving Tony Jones. One time, he was told that he needed to blade for Abdullah The Butcher and he refused. Lazie says about the incident:

"Everybody within a mile of the ring when Abby's in there - whether you're in the ring crew, a wrestler, or someone else - you're going to get color. Abby really cuts you legit. Tony had the mindset that he was a pure wrestler and he should've done what was right for the company."

XPW brought in random names, such as The Tonga Kid, Mustafa Saed, and Missy Hyatt, durings its early days to attract attention. Tonga Kid and Mustafa participated in Westsiders storylines, while Hyatt, who was brought in by Big Dick, was paired with Webb as his on-camera valet during her few appearances. In her Wrestling Universe shoot interview, she used the word "uneventful" three separate times (as well as the word "dull") to describe Webb, adding that while "he works hard," he also "had no personality - the personality of my fur coat--No, my fur coat has more personality than Johnny Webb!" Webb has jokingly referred to Hyatt as his "mom" in interviews, referencing how much older she was than him.

Hyatt told viewers of her Wrestling Universe shoot interview in regard to XPW's *Hardcore Conception* video, "Whatever you do, don't buy it because they didn't pay me for this, and they put us all on here." She later clarified to me that she had been paid for her live appearances in XPW, but hadn't been told she would be featured on any tape after the fact, and that her not being paid claim referred to her tape appearance.

As XPW garnered success, it also garnered attention from potential investors. One of these investors was Barry Mendelson, who was also a concert promoter, who supposedly was unsuccessful in his attempts to invest in or even buy ECW. Kleinrock, without mentioning Mendelson's name, said in his 2003 SCU interview:

"There was a group of investors from New York who wanted to, they told us at that point in time, buy into XPW. As we moved along, we found out based on the contract they were really trying to steal XPW. They were going to try and get the name and library and everything. It was not an investment. They were basically trying to give us a loan we were never going to be able to pay back. But the guy who was in charge of this group of investors had run arenas all over the country and had these incredible hook ups. So we went into the LA Sports Arena. I think we paid $2,000 to rent that building. Just for comparison, when [we] were at the [Grand] Olympic, I think we paid $10,000 just to walk in the door. So we had a smoking deal."

Kleinrock recounted the story similarly in August 2019 on facebook, saying, "Barry offered a loan to XPW but it was like if we were late 1 day by 1 dollar on 1 payment they would own the company." Lazie agrees with most of what Kleinrock says, including that Mendelson got XPW the LA Sports Arena for a very cheap price. Lazie goes so far as to call Mendelson a "shyster" who finances a company and then simply writes checks on the company's credit. He elaborated by saying that contrary to what Kleinrock said, Mendelson was on the West coast, but the "companies" that he insisted he financed were on the East coast. Lazie says that Extreme Associates employee Jon Blatt did a background search on Mendelson and found out about his shady history, so XPW distanced itself from him, but not before he was mentioned as part of a storyline on-screen and by Douglas in a WrestleLine.com interview as being in charge of XPW contract negotiations.

Part of XPW contracts involved exclusivity. XPW wrestlers could only wrestle for XPW in the So-Cal area. Kleinrock has said in interviews that there was no way they could justify charging $80 to see a talent at an XPW show one week and then letting them wrestle for another promotion up the road for $10 or $15. Black explained on his April 1, 2020 podcast why in his opinion the exclusivity clause was both fair and justified:

"We were paying guys more than they were making combined on the indie scene, so when I'm paying guys $100 or $150 to do a show, they were lucky if they were making $40 from these indies...I'm spending tens of thousands of dollars for a show, trying to make a real company. We have television. We have a lot of things that all of these other indies don't have, and I need to make these shows somewhat special to the local audience that are paying to come to the show."

Several wrestlers declined signing exclusive deals and continued wrestling locally for whoever would book them. Blood once said to Black that he should let them work elsewhere, prompting Black (according to Blood) to look at Hernandez as if to say, "This guy is gonna be trouble." Kaos also mentioned to me that he remembered Blood not getting along with Black and making it known that he wanted to work other shows besides XPW.

Blood was a perfect example of one of the versatile wrestlers who was a part of XPW's early days and showed that it was more than just hardcore. Along with Damien Steele, it seems that he was to be the main homegrown star of the company, judging by the fact that he was put over Supreme on the first show. Blood, meanwhile, seemed to be the person Black hyped in a June 30, 1999 interview with Gen Ross as "the Tommy Dreamer-type guy" who was yet to be named at that time. "He's hardcore, he bleeds, he sweats and dies to carry on the name XPW," Black said of him. "He's a high flyer and brawler."

Granted, Kleinrock said on Xtreme Memories that "at first, the very, very first few months, it really was 'Let's give the West coast an ECW-flavored show.'...If ECW had just broken three tables on a show, we were gonna break four." However, there was more to it than that. The UFO cross-promotion offered MMA-style athleticism that would become popular in the mainstream in later years. Daniels and the other APW talent offered a welcome dose of technical talents. In fact, on the same show as Daniels was a lucha tag team match by the stars of So-Cal's upstart Revolution Pro organization. Blood, meanwhile, the short-lived "Mr. XPW," offered a bit of every style. During the early days of the company, Kaos and Carlito even showed their commitment to wrestling hard by, before each show, doing a "full on 15 minute...dark match, just to get loosened up." While Black was intent on topping the hardcore aspects of ECW in the early days, he and his wrestlers were also willing to import alternative forms of athleticism into the product in order to make it a variety show.

4. Curveball marketing strategies

Any publicity was good publicity to XPW management. As Kloss said on the Barbwire-Press.com "Deep Impact" podcast, "One thing they can never criticize us for is for being afraid to do something because we were not afraid to do anything, and a lot of the times that bit us--we shot ourselves in the foot." In many respects, XPW's brass didn't care what onlookers said about it, as long as it was being discussed. Kaos told Kloss on Xtreme Memories that "People loved to hate XPW...It wasn't just East coast fans. There [were] West Coast fans that hated XPW." Kloss followed that by saying "You either loved or hated it."

While some people have said that sticking it to ECW was a priority for XPW, Shane Douglas has seemed to disagree in interviews, indicating that Black wanted to mirror ECW rather than impugn Heyman's company. Douglas said on an October 8, 2019 *Franchised with Shane Douglas* podcast that "At least on the overt level, it seemed like it wasn't like 'Hey, fuck ECW! We're here now.' What I was hearing Rob saying was 'I wanna be like ECW.'"

XPW's aspirations to live up to ECW's standards was itself a notable aspect of its promotional blueprint. Missy Hyatt also saw XPW as aspiring to be like ECW, but didn't put a positive spin on it like Douglas did. She told me that while she dealt with Big Dick Dudley (who got her into XPW) most of the time, on the rare occasions she interacted with Black, he resembled Heyman in that he was "hyper acting [with] ADD or ADHD...I just saw him running around at the TVs acting like Paul E." She made the same Heyman comparison in her Wrestling Universe shoot interview in 2001, where she described XPW as a "really low, low, low rent wannabe ECW."

While those two people painted Black's ambition to be like ECW as a positive (Douglas) and a negative (Hyatt), the more-blunt Josh Lazie, Black's former-business partner, says the same thing in a more matter of fact fashion - "If I had a nickel for every time Rob said 'This is how Paul would do it,' I would be rich."

Black no doubt took pride in the fact that, despite ECW having over a five-year head start in operation, XPW's home videos reached U.S. retail stores via Goldhil Home Video before ECW's did through Pioneer Entertainment. Kleinrock has said in interviews that XPW was largely sustained by hundreds of thousands of dollars in VHS and later DVD sales.

ECW and XPW talent ended up in the same building at ECW HeatWave 2000, as the XPW office bought some of its talent front row seats. Kloss said on the Kaos edition of Xtreme Memories that ECW tried to book the LA Sports Arena, but XPW already had that venue contractually secured. Black and Borden watched from home on Pay-Per-View. Going into the event, there were rumors that XPW would invade--on one web site, and there was even a report that Supreme and Sabu would do a run-in. In fact, Sabu wrote in his 2019 autobiography that Black asked him to participate in the stunt by attending the show, but he refused, and even advised Black that having his crew go was a bad idea. Around the same time, XPW and ECW were in the midst of a lawsuit. As part of the same case that involved ECW suing Sabu, they were also suing XPW for tortious interference with contractual relations and copyright, service mark, and trademark infringement (for use of the word "[E]xtreme").

Webb says that ECW "was expecting us" at HeatWave and had a plan going in, judging by the fact that they flew out Atlas Security instead of using the Grand Olympic Auditorium's in-house security. When I mentioned the HeatWave 2000 event to Atlas Security member Joe Wilchak at a CHIKARA show over a decade later, his first words were "Oh, yeah, [that was] the show with the riot!"

Webb said he had a front row seat, but that Kloss desperately wanted to be in the front row, so he gave up the seat and sat elsewhere with Westsider Chronic. Kloss said he'd let Webb sit front row later in the night and Webb thought about going to ask Kloss for his seat back at one point, but an Atlas Security team member was standing right behind him and told him not to even think about getting up. Webb remembers that he ended up outside, where several ECW wrestlers grabbed XPW ring crew members and were throwing them up against fences.

Jimmy and McMillan took some punches, with Jimmy having clumps of his hair pulled out that never grew back. Otherwise, though, the people who were beat up were members of the XPW ring crew, apparently including a female or two. One story that circulated was that a female who was pregnant was assaulted. Danny Doring admitted in his Kayfabe Commentaries *YouShoot* interview that women were being "dropped" (knocked down) in the parking lot. A YouTube comment in the 2010s indicated that ECW fansite ECWthugs.com posted pictures of the parking lot brawl that a fan took, although those photos didn't survive the evolution of the Internet and aren't anywhere to be found now. Heyman slapped Messiah, while XPW Asylum training school student Andre Verdun (Wrestling Society X's Youth Suicide), threw a stack of XPW flyers in Heyman's face.

Lazie says that ECW made the mistake of giving XPW press that night, and that this - turning negative publicity into positive publicity - was one of XPW's strengths. Kaos said on the September 22, 2020 So-Cal Pro Wrestling Podcast, "Immediately, the next day, XPW was known worldwide from that incident." On his LinkedIn profile, Kleinrock calls the event "one of the greatest publicity stunts in pro wrestling history." In July 2016, WWE posted a YouTube video about the incident titled "The night ECW fought off outlaw invaders." Black, in an e-mail the week that YouTube video went up, wrote that XPW got hundreds of thousands of dollars of free advertising from the incident and that even years later, people still remembered and discussed it. Messiah recalled to SMV that "We were getting recognized more there [by ECW HeatWave attendees] than we did at our own fucking shows."

XPW arguably got the last laugh with respect to HeatWave in a few ways. For instance, the night of HeatWave at the ECW wrestlers' hotel, Sandman, according to a Leroy The Ring Crew facebook post on May 6, 2020, "asked [XPW Asylum trainees] if we could watch a shopping bag full of Budweiser for him while he went into the bar for a shot. We said 'Sure,' and as soon as he was out of eyesight, we stole the beer and shared it with everyone the next day at the Asylum." Also, Black purchased a full page ad in World Of Wrestling (WOW) Magazine in the form of a letter addressed to Heyman, which GQ has said in interviews was what first made him attentive toward the idea of joining XPW. Additionally, many ECW wrestlers would call the Extreme Associates office asking for XPW bookings.

Following HeatWave, there was even a confrontation between Lazie and ECW wrestler Chilly Willy on an Internet wrestling podcast. Lazie had been a guest earlier in the show and had been listening in to Chilly's interview where he decried XPW. Lazie called back in and the show's host told Chilly that "the manager of Sabu" was on the line. Chilly apparently only heard "Sabu" and uttered "Sabu?!" in a seemingly shocked manner before the moderator clarified for him that it was Sabu's handler. The encounter generated this exchange:

Chilly Willy: "The next time we come out there, you bring your boys out--whoever you want. You bring your biggest boy out there and we'll issue a challenge right here nationally. I will take them on, whoever it may be."

Josh Lazie: "First of all, let's be real about this, Chilly. ECW's not coming back out here."

Chilly Willy: "No, because we made our point."

Josh Lazie: "Yeah, you made your point that you had to give away tickets for half a house."

Most people would never have called back into the show, but Lazie doing so was representative of XPW always wanting to pick a fight and generate chatter whenever possible.

XPW's determination to contravene ECW's legacy also showed itself in its decision to head to Philadelphia, ECW's stomping ground. The decision to move East was a double-edged sword, like many public relations game plans of XPW. Granted, it exposed them to fans in a new market. However, on the flip side, not all of the original XPW fans were still there to support the company when it returned to California for two shows in early 2003; some West coast fans felt that XPW abandoned them by running in Philly for six consecutive months. The decision to move East also was not supported by certain talent. GQ discussed the East-bound move in a May 1, 2008 Rubber Guard Radio interview:

"I was very instrumental in pushing for the original move to Philly for a *one*-time show. Going to Philly wasn't a stupid idea...if it was done how it should've been done, which was go do that show, the one show, come back to California, and then go back [to Philly] there three months later...That was really what the intent is, instead of making it a monthly move to Philly...Shane [Douglas] was in Black's ear all the time wanting to do the East coast thing."

Kloss told me that going to Philly resulted in "neglect" of the West coast fans and said on Barbwire-Press.com's "Deep Impact" podcast, "The company pretty much just took the whole So-Cal...fanbase for granted...[and] didn't really realize...that they had something very special in LA." Angel and Supreme also criticized the Philly move during In Your Head interviews, with Angel saying in August 2009 that "[Rob] put all the money on the East coast and forgot all about the West coast. We had fans here. We had a lot of fans, and we shouldn't have left them." Similarly,

Supreme said in 2012, "We were doing a good thing out here and we had a good fanbase and we went out there for no reason and it's like we're flying all these West coast wrestlers out there, which makes no sense at all...XPW should've stayed out here and we should've appreciated wrestling out here."

Lazie also disagreed with company decisions at times, and he was especially vocal, which led to him leaving the management side of the company at one point in 2001, and eventually the entire company altogether, along with Sabu. The disagreements tended to start with good intentions, but would get complicated when Lazie and Black saw the methods of attaining certain positive ends for XPW differently. For example, Sabu and Lazie had many creative ideas that Black would decline. Lazie adds that Black originally wanted Borden to manage Sabu, which others (including Sabu) didn't want. When Lazie was decided on instead, there was talk of calling him"Lazie-Abdul-Faarooq" as a takeoff on one of The Original Sheik's managers.

Lazie, along with Sabu, made efforts to develop working relationships with other promotions on XPW's behalf. For instance, they brought Stampede promoter Bruce Hart to Go Funk Yourself as a guest. Bruce joked in his Canadian accent to Rizzono that night that "The Gigolo"'s hardway cut from the sword (which he and Kaos had to use when Rizzono couldn't get his blade off his wrist) looked like a "little road rash from a bike accident," which amused Rizzono. Rivera said in 2020 that one of his all-time favorite memories in wrestling is Bruce saying to him, "Hey man, I love your gimmick. If you were up in Calgary, you'd have a job." According to Kaos and Lazie, Bruce had a meeting set up with Black at the EA office. He ended up waiting two hours for Black, who no-showed. Lazie was annoyed that Black treated Bruce like that and says that the Hart family member had been all for a deal between XPW and Stampede until that point.

Also, Sabu and Lazie stayed in Japan for about two weeks after they were scheduled to return to the U.S. in order to meet with AJPW officials and FMW owner Shoichi Arai about interpromotional dealings with XPW and perhaps running XPW shows in Japan, which Lazie says came "super close" to happening.

Lazie and Sabu ate dinner with Masato Tanaka at the Hard Rock Cafe in Tokyo and met Arai over lunch in Tokyo and LA. Lazie - who says he nearly had a physical confrontation with Steve Corino at a convention once - says that Hayabusa and Tanaka "had every single intention of working for" XPW in California, but that Black messed up the plans. The October 15, 2000 *Wrestling Observer* newsletter even reported that Tanaka had heat on him in the ECW locker room for agreeing to work for XPW.

These FMW interpromotional dealings not going further than they did is one of Lazie's biggest regrets about XPW. Lazie said that Hayabusa as the FMW champion would have had a year-long feud with Sabu, the XPW champion, around the world, leading to a one-on-one title match at the LA Sports Arena, with Atsushi Onita, Tanaka, Terry Funk, and Nosawa involved somehow in the angle, as well. Lazie presented the idea to Black and swears that Black responded, "Who is Hayabusa?" Lazie said that at that point, he realized it was hopeless. There was also going to be a Sabu vs. Funk vs. Onita match in XPW. Supreme, Myst, Jimmy, and Pogo ended up touring FMW, with Supreme and Jimmy even winning the promotion's tag team titles.

XPW also joined ECW, WWE, and CZW, on the bandwagon of failed negotiating to hold an exploding ring match in the U.S. with Onita. The FMW founder came to U.S. soil to do a press conference angle for the match. Lazie says Black met Onita an hour before the press conference, while Sabu and Lazie had been having meetings with him in Japan and the U.S. for weeks leading up to it and that Onita was going to do the match as a favor to Sabu.

Black ultimately stated in a fax he sent to Onita that was posted on the Internet that the explosion match couldn't happen due to Sabu's contractual dispute with ECW. Lazie told me, Rizzono said in a November 13, 2000 interview by Peter Hinds, and Kleinrock mentioned in a March 2021 Facebook post that there were also financial challenges as far as bringing in Onita's pyro crew. Lazie recalls that there were problems finding a venue for the match, too, and Rizzono and Kikuzawa add that when a venue (in LA) *was* found, the rules of the local city government for such a match were too stringent. Kikuzawa states that XPW discussed a booking fee with Onita and that Black "did everything for Onita he could," providing Onita with a five-star hotel, business class flight, etc. Kikuzawa references Black's fax by saying that Black "sent a kind message" to Onita saying "We are so sorry," and says that Onita "understood," accepted Black's apology, and had no negative feelings toward XPW.

One of the main ways XPW got backlash for HeatWave and the announced but never-to-happen Sabu-Onita explosion match was via the Internet. AVN.com in the early days and GeneRossExtreme.com and Extreme Associates.com at various times throughout XPW's existence covered the wrestling promotion's news, and Ross' site conducted interviews with XPW on-camera talents such as Messiah, Jimmy, and GQ.

Additionally, as early as 1999 and until 2001, podcasts were posted in RealPlayer Media (.ram) format on XPWrestling.com by original webmaster Tony T., before podcasts in their traditional, mainstream form existed. The weekly audio shows included audio coverage from XPWs shows with Kloss on play-by-play, as well as interviews with XPW characters. Tony would post the audio stream and multi-page galleries of backstage (posed) and in-ring action photos from most XPW live events on the web site before he went to bed around 4-5 am the morning following the previous night's show. Tony recalls that he was able to do this because he had good time management skills, "access to great software," was "fluent" with "web technology" like RealPlayer, and had "high speed internet with fast upload speed" for the era. "I had pretty much free reign to shoot video and audio interviews with the wrestlers," he recalls. Perhaps the most high-profile feature Tony did was his 1999 interview with then-XPW talent Nicole Bass, as she told all about her sexual harassment lawsuit against WWE. Black set up the sit-down with Tony and Bass cried at times during the emotional sit-down. Tony said in 2020 that Black later, after Tony left, told him that "Kevin didn't like my work, but he did and couldn't override Kevin."

When Tony's time in the company had run its course, web-mastering duties of the XPW site - as well as ExtremeAssociates.com - began rotating between Inkyo Volt Hwang (a.k.a. Chico Wanker Wang a.k.a. "Voltron"), who passed away about half a decade later in a controversial story on porn gossip sites, and GQ. Wang, Tony says, "reluctantly took over the" XPW site, as he wasn't a wrestling guy. During Wang's and GQ's era as webmasters, the sites, especially ExtremeAssociates.com, posted controversial gossip and news stories which were editorialized in such a way as to make them excessively salacious and wild. GQ also was the webmaster of his own site, GQMoney.com, which promoted his endeavors, and by proxy, some XPW developments, too. With Tony no longer involved, XPWrestling.com also started moving away from audio multimedia at this point.

The frequency of columns on XPWrestling.com really started picking up in 2001. A lot of the content on these in-house web sites from 2001 to 2002 was written by GQ with inspiration from Black. GQ himself authored columns called "The Money Shot" and more frequently, "Diggin' Up Dirt Bert," where he posted XPW gossip. For instance, an early 2002 "Bert" column hinted that a power player would be coming into XPW to challenge Black, and sure enough, a few months later, Douglas made his return and forced Black out of XPW storylines. GQ confirmed to me in September 2003 that the "Bert" column reference was indeed to Douglas. During the build-up to Hostile Takeover, GQ, as "Bert," acknowledged CZW, 3PW, and ROH by name and encouraged East coast fans to give XPW's product a shot.

Kleinrock also wrote a "From the Desk of the VP" column, which candidly discussed XPW-relevant topics like the wrestling media's criticism of the company and the quest for national XPW TV syndication clearance, as well furthered XPW storylines and narrative, sometimes in favor of the Black Army stable (which he was a member of) and sometimes from a neutral perspective, where he'd acknowledge the talent of Black Army adversaries. In this early 2000s era, before blogging and social media became popular, there were also a few columns written by wrestlers.

ExtremeAssociates.com and XPWrestling.com even saw storylines developed. For instance, on March 27, 2002, ExtremeAssociates.com theatrically announced that Black had suffered a stroke and was in the hospital. The web site's account was inconsistent, as its April 2 report that he suffered "minor paralysis to the right side of his body" changed on April 24 without explanation to his "left side." The site gave a street address for fans to send sympathy cards to and when he "returned" from the hospital, posted groggy pictures of a wheelchair-bound Black to boot, depicting him in a recovery state. The stroke angle was also featured on XPW TV.

Perhaps the most talked about publicity stunt in XPW history happened in February 2002 when EA announced plans to feed a small dog, Bruiser, to a snake on a members-only section of their web site. Angel recalled that Rob absolutely adored the dog, but in order to rile up folks, Wang posted pictures of the dog in an electric chair and wrote salacious stories about him being fed nutritious food to fatten him up. Wang later issued a long statement saying that EA's office had been raided by local animal rights groups, and that Black had been beaten to a bloody pulp while refusing to give up the dog. While some animal rights organizations did contact and even come to the office, police never brutalized Black "in a scene reminiscent of the Rodney King beatings," as ExtremeAssociates.com's dramaticized rants about the "Los Angeles Gestapo" claimed.

As GQ told me in March 2003, "there was no intention to feed any puppy to the snake and people who believed that we were were out of their heads…Our site focused on the ridiculous, out there, and insane." That being said, Angel recalls that at least one live chicken was fed to the snake at the office, and was taped; as part of an XPW TV vignette for Crimson, a version of that footage was aired that was so blurry that it was hard to tell what it was, so it went over the heads of most people. However, the snake and dog incident got XPW on the front pages of plenty of wrestling news sites, so in XPW management's eyes, the intended mission had been accomplished. GQ says:

"[Rob] had no involvement whatsoever [in the dog and snake stunt]. Rob had pretty much given free reign of the website to [Wang]...and that was a publicity stunt done by that webmaster. And it was damn good. That webmaster had talent, and that's why Rob trusted him. Pet people and animal cops were at the office. And they were like, 'We need to see the dog,' and then you'd hear the PA system go off with someone yelling, 'The dog is dead. The snake just ate him.' It was really funny...The dog got a lot of love from everybody, as all the animals that are at the office do...We had a real snake, and turtles, and fish, and other dogs."

Even Shane Douglas denigrated the dog and snake angle in his Wrestling-News.com interview building up to Hostile Takeover, bringing it up without being asked about it:

"I beat [Black's] ear on that at the time. I was very close to signing with him and that knocked me off his roster for about two--two and a half months before I would even talk to him again. And he understands that. He knows it was wrong, but looking back at it, he didn't at that time have enough business savvy to the wrestling business to know not to say that. He thought it would be controversial and draw attention…[He was] totally classless and wrong for doing it."

One publicity stunt that Black was entirely in on was his 2001 run for Los Angeles mayor. Wang's RobBlackForMayor.com web site had little choice but to acknowledge his porn involvement, though it tried to paint a softer picture of the content, saying that he directed "movies specifically intended to elevate the mind and encourage discourse" and which provided a "depiction of those Americans who are often ignored." A segment specifically about Black and his campaign aired on Jon Stewart's The Daily Show on Comedy Central, although it focused on the porn rather than XPW. Black credits the XPW street team with a lot of the success of the campaign, saying on Will Carroll's September 2019 TeenSetRadio podcast, "I was able to do it because I had a street team. At any one time, I had 30-40 people out there canvassing--getting signatures." Black placed eleventh out of 15 other mayoral candidates.

XPW's fanbase spread the word about XPW not only as a street team, but also by launching over 20 fansites. XPW's heyday was at the peak of the "wrestling fan sites" era. Most of the fan sites were divisions of other bigger wrestling sites at the time and had simply registered an "xpw" domain name, but their sub-pages were either part of the bigger wrestling site, or were hosted on web site creation services from the era. XPW1.com and StrictlyXPW.com were notable exceptions which were hosted on their own domain name server and had their own sub-pages on those same .com domains. XPW fan sites included:

1.   XPWTV.com

2.   XPW1.com (folded around late 2001)

3.   XPWlive.com (xpwlive1.tripod.com, xpwlive0.tripod.com, xpwlive2001.cjb.net, xpwlive1.homestead.com, xpwlive.caliwrestlinglive.com, among other URLs; ran by future wrestler Shiima Xion/DJ Z/Joaquin Wilde, as well as Glen Carambas and Will Tha K)

4.   Blood, Beers, & Titties a.k.a. XtremePro.cjb.net a.k.a. Biazza.org/Xtreme (according to two sources, the first XPW fan site ever made)

5.   StrictlyXPW.com (ran by Oscar Pierce, Jr.)

6.   GotXPW.com (a part of WrestlingNation.com)

7.   XPWhardcore.com (xpwrestlinghardcore.hypermart.net)

8.   XPWxtreme.com (XPWxtreme.tripod.com)

9.   XP-F'n-W (geocities.com/xp_fn_w/)

10.   XPWMedia.com (2002-XPW's folding)

11.   Now That's Xtreme (ThatsXtreme.cjb.net)

12.   All XPW (http://www.oe-pages.com/SPORTS/Wrestling/xpw/)

13.   XPWfanz.net (unclear whether this was simply an alternate URL of XPWTV.com or if it was an entirely separate fansite)

14.   XPWnews.com (a part of WrestlingSolutions.com; active in 2001; ran by Aaron Saxton, Ethan "EMAXSAUN" Feldman, Jason Xa, Shawn Vaughn, & Wynn Carlson)

15.   XPWForever.com (http://members.home.net/xpwforever/xpw.htm)

16. XPW2THAMAX (prowrestlingandstuff.homestead.com/index.html)

17. XPWShillSquad.com

18. XPWcity.tk

19. XPWwrestling.de (German fan site)

20. XPWpro.com (ran by Sean Widup)

21. HouseOfXtreme.com (towards the end of XPW; another Sean Widup fan site)

22. & 23. two angelfire web sites by the real-life brothers who would become indie wrestlers Louis Lyndon ("LWorld's XPW Wrestling") and Flip Kendrick ("XPW Revolution"/"DWorld's XPW").

There was also "The Alternative XPW Messageboard" during some of the California era. XPW personalities had their own web sites: LizzyBordenXPW.com (which was, like XPWNews.com, part of WrestlingSolutions.com), the rare, if ever, updated HomelessJimmy.com, and "The Hardcore Homo"'s AngelXSane.com.

The three most popular and active fansites were likely XPW1.com, XPWlive.com, and XPWTV.com. XPW1.com featured multimedia as well as daily newsboard posts. It was the site that leaked that Messiah had left the company after having an affair with Borden. A year after his firing, Billy would return to Los Angeles only to be assaulted in his apartment by two assailants losing his thumb. The two men escaped the scene and have never been caught or even identified. Messiah has gone on record many times as stating straight out that he believes Black organized the attack. A statement posted on XPWrestling.com that week stated, in part: "XPW sends its most sincere thoughts and prayers to The Messiah. The incident of the other night is a tragedy no matter what has been said in the past and no matter where feelings stand right now." The post also included a link for fans to send "get well wishes" to Messiah.

Most people believe that Black was behind the "hit," while some people argue otherwise. An anonymous worker states, "I mentioned the 'suspects' list (Kristi's then husband, Jessica Darlin's husband Bobby, etc.) and it was pretty much said to just show how all roads point to only one man. The ONLY one he really ever had heat with. I don't [know] if Rob had anything to do with Billy's attack, but I really don't think anyone else on my list had ever thought about Billy in a negative way."

Chris Hamrick is more positive about Messiah, and was in touch with him for a period following the accident, but says he doubts Black was involved: "I personally don't think Rob is dumb enough to have it done. First of all, he knows he would be the number one suspect. Also, why would he risk losing everything he has worked for on doing something like that? Rob is way smarter than that." He reiterated this viewpoint in his Bert Duckwell shoot interview around 2003.

Shane Douglas said in his 2003 RF Video shoot interview that he once asked Black point-blank about the rumors. Douglas said that Black said something along the lines of how he wouldn't risk his freedom and he would never have been able to keep it quiet if he had been behind it, since he's so braggadocious.

As a result of the attack, Messiah became careful about who he associated with. He admitted in an interview done shortly after the attack (an interview which ironically was conducted by Yap) that one of these people was Chris Hamrick. In the same interview, he said that Kaos and Hamrick were the only people from XPW to call him to see how he was doing after the attack. Hamrick told Duckwell that Messiah was confiding in him shortly after the incident and then "like a week later" told him "'Don't take this wrong, but I can't talk to you" because "you work for that company" (XPW).

Messiah would go on to work for rival extreme wrestling company Combat Zone Wrestling (CZW) in the years to come, forging his career as a deathmatch wrestler taking on the likes of Sick Nick Mondo, John Zandig, Homicide and countless others (while forming friendships with other ex XPW talent like Luke

Hawx who were recruited) and getting happily married with children for the years to follow.

XPWlive.com tended to be more of a gossip web site with lackluster grammar, and even acknowledged the EA side of business at times. It started to become critical of XPW during the later days and even became a fansite for cross-town rival EPIC Pro Wrestling, changing its name to "EPIClive," prompting Kleinrock to send the web site a letter that read, in part:

"Fan sites are one thing, but some often go beyond the call... a site that has the name XPW in it and uses the company's trademarked name is really being granted permission by XPW... and there is a line we have drawn. Sites that are supportive of XPW and only feature XPW news and info will be allowed to use the XPW name. Sites that feature outside news, trash talking, and more importanty unauthorized images (from adult movies) and sell tapes that are illegal... what I'm getting at is that if XPWlive would like to continue to flourish, then those in charge need to make a decision on whether to continue on the path they're on... or keep XPWlive, keep supporting the cause, and get on board with the program."

XPW management was doing what they could to crack down on public criticism, which is further evidenced by XPWTV.com becoming, in the words of a May 1, 2002 joint press release between it and XPWrestling.com, an official "subsidiary affiliate" of and the "official fansite of XPW." XPWTV.com was run by Jonathan Siderman and his big brother, Slava "OG" Siderman (now in charge of the newly revived XPW's photography) and stuck mostly to XPW coverage, and also involved contributors Sean McCartney and "El Diablo." It featured a newsboard, TV recaps (which were also posted on the official XPW web site), and XPWTV.com-exclusive content such as XPW wrestler and personality interviews and music videos. For instance, when Larry Rivera left XPW, the younger Siderman did a candid phone interview with him discussing his departure outside of kayfabe and posted it on XPWTV.com. Rivera said in 2020 that he had been "anxious to get [his] story out" about why he left XPW.

XPWTV.com also featured the most active XPW message board, which survived after XPW's folding until 2006. By that point, it had become WTFBoards.com, although it still housed all of the old XPW-related posts. Additionally, XPWTV.com released a DVD which featured fancam footage as part of a fan contest. While some of that DVD's contents are now on YouTube decades later, the prize contained what at the time was rare media, such as candid footage of the wrestlers and fancam music videos of angles such as Sandman's debut, which never aired on XPW TV. Full XPW TV episodes were even posted on XPWTV.com (as well as XPWrestling.com and StrictlyXPW.com at times), often in RealPlayer format, and it would take hours to download them back then. XPWTV.com also conducted a shoot interview with Vic Grimes, although only two clips from it ever saw the light of day.

Jonathan got involved with XPWrestling.com and continued the trend of Tony T. by posting extensive photo galleries from each event from mid-2001 until the Philly run began. He also did graphic design work for the official XPW site and ran play-by-play coverage on pages that could be updated live as shows happened. When asked in a June 2002 interview on XPWTV.com's message board if he considered himself an employee of XPW, he said " I'm a dedicated, hard-working, volunteer." In later years, though, both Sidermans ended up directing for EA, with Jonathan known as "Ricky D." ("Dynamite") and Slava as "Ivan E. Rection." Angel said that the Sidermans were two of the very few fans that Black didn't mind kayfabe being broken around because he knew that they had a good thing going with XPWTV.com. In addition to their roles on XPWTV.com and XPWrestling.com, Slava and primarily Jonathan also operated XPWShillSquad.com, a virtual street team site. In the same June 2002 interview, Jonathan said that on a typical day XPW has a show, "I get home at 2am, upload images from the show, and send the show...recap world-wide to various Internet wrestling sites. I go to sleep around 5am."

Internet coverage backfired on XPW more than a few times. Sabu's debut was leaked online by Black prematurely. SCU's Steve Bryant spoiled the news of Douglas' return in July 2002 before the "Night Of Champions" show and says an angry Rob Black called him about it trying to get him to give up the identity of the leaker.

Joey Styles' debut was leaked online before it happened. In January 2003, Justice Pain called his former-CZW boss John Zandig and told him that he had successfully negotiated to join XPW. It leaked onto CZWWrestling.com before his debut appearance on XPW TV aired.

All of these qualities, from public ambitions to mirror ECW to bragging about getting sued to Black's mouth (and posts on his web sites) getting him and XPW in trouble, contributed to XPW's advertising strategies. For a period, fans who navigated to ExtremeAssociates.com and didn't want to accept the warning for explicit content could click "No" and be redirected to the XPW web site, so either way they were giving Black their business. Through XPWrestling.com, XPW-related coverage on ExtremeAssociates.com and GeneRossExtreme.com, and a large network of fansites, XPW possessed a vibrant Internet presence ahead of its time that both got its name out in interactive ways and shot it in the foot at times. Attempts to extend the olive branch to international promotions for networking and working relationships showed interest in acquiring awareness from fans overseas, but the plans often didn't pan out ideally. In-person local Los Angeles-area publicity stunts like HeatWave 2000 and Rob Black's mayoral candidacy tried to make the best of bad coverage. XPW didn't always get positive press, but they didn't care, as long as the company was the focus of the media attention.

8. Pushing The Physical Envelope

Rob Black's company was called "**Xtreme Pro Wrestling**" for a reason - many stunts were over the top and aimed to outdo ECW, whose in-ring antics were already beyond the pail. Many XPW personalities have even admitted as much in interviews. Altar Boy Luke has said multiple times, including in a 2019 interview with Sam Roberts, that "[Black] had no...compassion for somebody else's life, for somebody else's health. Everything is 'If you can't do it, we'll get somebody else in that spot.'"

On his April 15, 2020 podcast, Black responded to Luke's claims by saying "I didn't force anybody" to do perilous stunts and pointed out that Luke's son did a comparatively dangerous wrestling physical exploit in February 2020. Black also responded to this idea on his May 8, 2020 podcast, saying:

"If there was something that I wanted to put out there, and a wrestler or whoever didn't want to do it, I would give them the option, and then I would find someone else, but as far as spots go, [if] somebody didn't feel comfortable doing a spot, I wouldn't say 'You gotta do it!'…[Do] you know how many spots would be done and I'd be screaming in my speaker piece to Patrick Hernandez, our referee, or Danny Ramirez, the other referee, saying…'Is he alright?! Give me a sign. Rub your ear…I know I was perceived as a monster, but that was furthest, and I mean furthest, from who I am and who I was back then. I never wanted the boys to get hurt…I never rubbed my hands together and said 'Oh ya, maybe they'll get maimed.' And when things did go bad and somebody did get hurt, I would completely question everything that we were doing."

Steele, who says he didn't always get along with Black, defends Black now on this front, saying about the stunts, "Rob didn't have to coax anybody. Everybody did it on their own" because "everybody wants to be famous." One person who exemplified this idea was "The Hardcore Homo," who said on a May 2008 Rubber Guard Radio, "I wanted to make a name for myself. I didn't care what happened to my body to do it" because "in my head, there was no consequences...I always thought 'I'm gonna be fine.'" He added an example, saying "Back in the XPW days, I wouldn't think twice about jumping off a 40 foot scaffold, and made the interesting observation that "Really, I only had three or four death matches in my career, but when I did do them, I went balls out."

Luke also admits in hindsight that he was naive about his safety at times. He said on "Xtreme Memories" in September 2020 that he considers himself "foolish" for doing some dangerous antics, but that "I had nothing to lose" back then when "building a name for myself." Homeless Jimmy was another example of having no fear during the XPW days, as Webb said on Rubber Guard Radio that "The first thing I hear the next day [after New Jack's XPW dive] is how bummed out Jimmy is because now the bar has been raised. As soon as that [dive] went down, [Jimmy] was foaming at the mouth to top it." Angel went so far as to say on "Xtreme Memories" that "How nobody ever died in XPW is amazing."

Some people didn't specialize in hardcore wrestling stunts, but found themselves asked to partake nonetheless. For instance, Kraq was penciled in against Vic Grimes for the second death match tournament. He had been hoping he could just stay a bodyguard and be the one who wrestles and doesn't bleed. Amazed that XPW used real barbed-wire and light bulbs and wondering how the guys wrestled with blood in their eye, he watched some XPW death matches and thought to himself, "Do you really want to go through that?" Black walked Kraq through what he needed from him in the match vs. Grimes, and after all this time of saying to himself that he wouldn't do death matches, he told Black that it'd be no problem, as he didn't want to disappoint his boss ("I think had Rob not asked me and it was anybody else, I probably would've told them 'No,' but because it was Rob, I said 'Yeah.'" - Xtreme Memories).

He got through it unscathed. Grimes was to end the match by dropping Kraq onto a board with both sides wrapped in barbed-wire and told Kraq that there was a screw sticking out of one side and that he could paralyze him if he dropped him on that. So, Grimes turned the board over so Kraq wouldn't land on the screw. "Vic saved my ass," Kraq told me, and he called Grimes his favorite XPW opponent on Xtreme Memories.

"Playboy" Buddy Rose, Rizzono's XPW manager, shared on an In Your Head Radio interview his observation about XPW that "A lot of the things they were doing were taking a toll on these kids' bodies." Steele admitted in an *LA New Times* article in 2000 that XPW death matches bordered "the masochist spectrum" and said that he doesn't teach death match wrestling at the Asylum training school: "That's nothing you need to teach. You basically go out there, and some guy throws you into barbed wire and you bleed." Kleinrock seemed prouder of XPW's violence, stating in a September 2001 interview with UCLA's *Daily Bruin* student newspaper "Our goal from the beginning was to bring hardcore wrestling to the West Coast. That is what we have done." As a result, XPW not surprisingly had its fair share of near catastrophic injuries in the ring.

Supreme would go onto become Mr. XPW and lead the company in the ring with his style of deathmatch wrestling, facing off against fellow colleagues Kaos, Steve Rizzono, Johnny Webb, and countless others. Billy on Supreme: "He and I would beat the shit out of each other and we loved every minute of it. Being good friends out of the ring just made us hit each other harder. I know It makes no sense." Supreme gave his body to XPW and the workers/fans all thanked him for it. Supreme would go onto be inducted into the 2021 GCW Deathmatch Hall Of Fame posthumously.

For instance, Supreme suffered second degree burns over much of his body from a fire stunt gone wrong that resulted from an idea that Supreme said in a 2012 In Your Head interview he and his nephew, Kaos, came up with. However, XPW mistakenly used charcoal fluid instead of lighter fluid, which caused the fire to be especially difficult to extinguish. Kloss mentioned in a mid-2000s era In Your Head interview and Rivera agreed in 2020 that the remnants of Supreme's "burnt flesh" could be smelled from "way up top at the Olympic" (Kloss' words). Supreme said on a December 29, 2002 Xtreme Mayhem Radio interview, "That accident was the most horrible thing that probably ever happened to me, and it wasn't just getting caught on fire; it was the whole getting over it--the scrubbing of my skin." Supreme said on an August 2009 In Your Head episode about the incident:

"I felt the heat before I even went through the table and then when I went through the table, I was trying to pat myself down on the mat and I realized it wasn't going off. I was on fire for 15 seconds...I ended up looking like Homer Simpson running around like a buffoon."

GQ explained in August 2003:

"That night was crazy, and it really depressed me....It was...every bit as serious as it looked. I remember going to see him at the burn unit ward of the hospital the next day. I had to put on the gloves, and gown, AND HAT...Supreme's reaction [to it] was mellow. But Supreme always kept most of his emotions to himself. He would always rib me, because he knew I felt guilty and bad about it...The next few weeks on TV, Kaos, VC and me were talking mad shit about Supreme while roasting various things on a Bar-B-Q. That made me feel bad. I know Supreme's kid really didn't like me, and

I understand why. I was like the biggest asshole in the world to his dad on TV, and it just made me feel bad all the time. But that's wrestling, I guess."

XPW's ring crew also got public flak for extinguishing the fire before they put out Supreme. However, Supreme - who suffered permanent scarring from the incident, but didn't get an arm graft, despite doctors' recommendations - defended the students in an August 20, 2002 Wrestling-News.com interview, saying "The problem was I rolled out another way, and all they saw is--[from their angle] they thought I was still in that big flame." GQ lays blame this way: "It was 100% the fault of whoever bought the wrong fluid, whoever didn't extinguish him right away, and then everyone in the company's fault for not double checking the fluid."

Supreme recalled to Wrestling-News.com how even he was surprised by a fan who gave him a knife to use on Crimson. Similarly, traditionally technical wrestler Vinnie Massaro, while wrestling the only death match of his XPW run (vs. Luke), was provided by a fan a piece of a light tube, inside of which was a kendo stick fragment, lemon juice, and fish hooks, according to Massaro's Xtreme Memories episode. Supreme and Massaro both declined to use the weapon each fan gave them on their opponent.

Another notorious incident besides Supreme catching on fire involved New Jack and Vic Grimes. When Grimes joined XPW, Black made them sit together and bury their heat from ECW, which stemmed from a botched scaffold fall in which Grimes landed on Jack, causing him permanent injuries. At that moment, Grimes told me, Jack even looked at him and said, "[Our incident in ECW] was a long time ago. Let's make this [program] work." Grimes agreed. Black said on his April 1, 2020 podcast, "We didn't have to separate them. New Jack never walked around and said 'One of these days, I'm gonna kill Vic.' Vic never came to me in my office and said 'You know, Rob, I have some concerns with New Jack." They worked together for about a year on camera and got along, with Grimes saying in 2019 that there was "just straight professionalism" from Jack.

Then came one of the most notorious independent wrestling matches of the modern era, Free Fall, in February 2002. It was a scaffold match, with the winner being the person to toss their opponent off of a tall structure. The day of the show, Grimes went up on the scaffold with Supreme before the show and the ring was moved in the direction of the turnbuckle he fell near, so that probably saved his life, as he hit that ring rope.

Also earlier that day, Jack pulled Rizzono into one of the private dressing rooms in the basement of the Grand Olympic Auditorium. Jack locked the door, turned the lights off, didn't say anything for about 10 seconds, and just stared at a confused Rizzono, who wondered if Jack was going to attack or use the chair in the corner of the room on him. Then Jack reached into his bag and pulled out a taser. He pressed a button on it and a blue laser shot out. He told Rizzono that he was going to kill Grimes. Rizzono thought, "Wow, this is going to be an interesting night." Jack also pulled Hamrick and Sandman into private rooms that day and gave them similar previews of what was to happen. "He said he wouldn't let go until the battery was done," Hamrick said.

Towards the end of the match, they climbed to the top of the scaffold. Grimes explained in his Awesome Bomb Fight Radio interview that they "were supposed to do some spots up there" on the scaffold. Instead, when they got up there, Jack pulled out the taser, which Grimes says "wasn't planned at all." Jack had acquired the taser by coercing Scott Snot into bringing him to a pawn shop earlier in the day. Grimes says, "I could kill Snot for it. Supposedly, Jack made him go do it and when Jack tells you to do something, you do it." In one of the most replayed images in pro wrestling history, Grimes took the bump off the scaffold through the tables.

Grimes says that his mother had come to the show, unbeknownst to him, and was at ringside for the match, which took place more than a couple hours from where she lived. When the bump happened, she abandoned her purse at her seat and started yelling at her son from as close as she could get, behind the ringside guardrail. He realized she was there and had to keep kayfabe, which he says wasn't easy. Some kids in the crowd returned her pocketbook to her after the ringside confrontation. He said on Xtreme Memories that she "had this custom Vic Grimes shirt she made, and she gave that to the kids" as thanks for bringing her back her purse.

After the fans left, Grimes said he had plenty of waivers to sign for refusing medical treatment beyond the bare minimum. When he got backstage, he said he thought he and Jack were going to fight for real. In his Awesome Bomb Fight Radio interview, he concurred with Jack's claims in shoot interviews: "He literally wanted to throw me off there for real and hurt me because of what happened in the past. He wanted to get back at me." He asked Jack what happened outside the locker room at Free Fall right after he got backstage, and Jack told him that "every day I pay for what you did [to] me [in Danbury]" due to injuries. Vic explained what happened from that point on:

"I go 'Man, all the crap that you've done and all the crap that I've done - it's enter at your own risk.' I go 'Fuck you, man. You know what's up' and I go 'And now you want to throw me off and really try to hurt me?' And he goes 'I was just trying to pay you back for the crap that I went through and this and that' and...he basically said that 'I've given you everything to try to hurt you. I've hit you the hardest I could with weapons. I've thrown you off the scaffolding and you're still standing here walking.' and he goes 'Bottom line is I've done everything to try to hurt you.' So I go, 'So now what?' and he says 'I could easily go to my car and get my gun and blast your ass, but I value my freedom.' And I go 'What's up, then?' and he actually stuck his hand out and shook my hand, and he says 'We're straight.'"

Even the girls were not exempt from dangerous stunts. Borden told Luke Y. Thompson of *The LA New Times* in 2000, "After a couple of days you get sore and you get bruises. It's the hardest thing I've done. I love it more than porno!" In 2003, Grimes was involved in an incident that saw him powerbomb Borden from the top turnbuckle to the outside of the ring in the direction of a ringside table that she largely missed. Her lung got punctured and as a result, she had to take a train home from Philadelphia to California because doctors were afraid her lung would collapse if she flew. She said in a May 2008 conversation that Black had been yelling in the cameraman's ear to pan the camera to ringside so it could get a clear shot of the bump, but he failed to do so in time and only caught Grimes tossing her, not the landing. Douglas says of the bump:

"Vic Grimes had never cleared it with me. Afterwards, he tried to say, 'Well, she said it was OK.' Well, she wasn't qualified to say whether it was OK or not...As the booker of the company I was extremely angry because A. we had a talent now out because of very stupid reasons and B. a girl who I like...could've seriously injured herself. I mean she did, but she could've permanently injured herself by doing that."

Douglas' words to me in 2006 were read to Grimes over a decade later in 2019. Grimes reiterated that Borden told him the powerbomb was fine to do on her and he thought that was sufficient because her husband was the owner of the company. Douglas said in his 2003 RF Video shoot interview, saying "She was willing to put her ass on the line and she thought she had to make up for her shortcomings in other ways." Grimes admits that both Black and Borden got more involved in the in-ring physical aspects of XPW than they should have been, and specifically mentioned that Tammy Lynn Sytch was more cut out for the physical aspect of wrestling than Borden.

Speaking of Sytch, her WCW back injury, she said in a December 2007 Wrestling Epicenter interview, was reaggravated in XPW when Grimes powerbombed her through a table. Sytch added in an In Your Head interview in June 2007 that she sustained "two herniated discs in [her] lower back" from that bump. She also shot on Grimes' mistake (in her opinion) in her 2006 RF Video shoot, saying that "since then, I have to go to a chiropractor three times a week and I have permanent nerve damage in my lower back."

Grimes also partook in violent XPW matches against Supreme. They wrestled each other in both a no-rope, barbed-wire match and an exploding ring death match (thanks to HutchFX's Robert Hutchins) in 2001. Grimes recalls that he could suggest anything and Supreme was willing to do it, telling me "Between the minds of the twisted, you can come up with anything." He even said on Ultraviolent Radio on February 16, 2011 that he and Supreme having "the same sick mind" caused them "to try to one-up each other all the time." He explains that Supreme was different than New Jack, in that Jack hardly ever wanted to do anything, and when he did, he just wanted to break stuff over your head, use weapons in obvious ways, and head home, whereas Supreme also wanted to use weapons, but in a unique way.

In the no-rope barbed-wire match, it became evident to Grimes that Supreme wore scars as badges of honor. Grimes told Kloss on Xtreme Memories that after Supreme spilled off the ladder to ringside, "as I cover him [at ringside], he literally right under his bicep, he's got fluorescent tubes stuck in his bicep, and he's looking at me" as Grimes covers him at ringside "and he goes 'Dude, look at that! Ain't that cool?!' And he's just like 'Oh man, look at that! That's cool!'..and he's laughing at it, and I'm like 'Yeah, that's pretty sick, man, but I ain't pulling that out!'" Meanwhile, Grimes remembers that during the explosion match, one of the C-4 plates exploded from his uranage on the floor onto Supreme and ravaged Grimes' arm, as well as gave him a concussion. He thought for a few moments that he had brain damage. The head issues lasted for about two weeks and he'd have to pull over for a few minutes while driving.

Grimes' hardcore wrestling experience led him to give advice to two upcoming XPW wrestlers about the risks of becoming too violent. One was fellow APW alum Steve Rizzono, who is one of few wrestlers to this day about two decades later to do a death match with just wrestling trunks on. Grimes says that Rizzono always wanted to do something extreme and be hardcore to get fan approval. He told Rizzono "That's not your gimmick" and that if he did it on occasion, the fans would always expect him to do it. Rizzono ended up in a wheelchair for over 10 years after XPW folded and underwent several surgeries. Grimes also gave similar advice to Angel, who he says "took it a little too far." He told Angel that the fans may pop for the wild stuff he does in the ring, but those fans wouldn't be there when he's in the hospital in his time of need.

Grimes mentioned on Xtreme Memories an ECW Arena match where his forehead was staplegunned. He misremembered his opponent as Supreme when it was really Douglas. Grimes mentioned to Kloss that since "they didn't have the small staples, and they had these thick ass long ones" that "stuck in so deep" that "a pair of pliers" were necessary to "pull them out...and they had to go one at a time and they broke off in my head." Douglas also stapled Grimes' tongue, and this was before Necro Butcher, JC Bailey, and others were doing that tongue stunt on a regular basis, so Grimes was one of the first to do it. He recalled on Xtreme Memories that " it went in so deep that when we went out and ate dinner later, I was trying to eat soup. My tongue started swelling up."

XPW had a King of the Deathmatch Championship, and three King of the Deathmatch Tournaments throughout its existence. Kaos told me, "It was either be in a deathmatch or not be on the show. I just wanted to wrestle that night. I never thought twice about it." Kaos told Kloss on the "Xtreme Memories" podcast in August 2020 that there was pressure on him: "[Management was] like 'Well, you better fucking bleed and if you don't bleed it's your ass.'"

The second tournament in 2001 was the night Rizzono became one of few wrestlers to this day decades later to do a Beds of Barbed-Wire & Thumbtacks death match (his first death match) in just trunks (no tights or shirt on), to Grimes' chagrin. It was a long weekend for Rizzono, as he wrestled Pogo and Grimes in a three-way the night before at an indie show in Northern California, before driving overnight to XPW. In an interview with Peter Hinds on February 24, three days before the tournament, Rizzono - when asked by Hinds how he would get through the upcoming weekend - joked "pharmaceutical help." He closed the interview by showing off his pristine forehead to the camera, saying "My head is clean now. Next week - [it'll be] swiss cheese."

Sure enough, an interview with Hinds a week later on February 27 opened with Rizzono showing off his back, littered with barbed-wire scratches and over 15 bandaid-sized gauzes, as well as other visibly fresh cuts on his right arm, hand, and forehead. Rizzono told Hinds that it was his "hardcore stupidity for the year" and "the best color I've ever got." At one point, Supreme had Irish whipped Pogo into him while he was already stuck in a crucified manner to a barbed-wire board, which Rizzono told me wasn't planned. Rizzono described that moment to Hinds as feeling like "a venus flytrap" of barbed-wire engulfed his body. He said he "blacked out" at a couple points during the match, after which he said he got a standing ovation backstage. Rizzono told Hinds he went to the hospital the following night (Sunday) to get checked out. Meanwhile, Rizzono told me that he got 12 or 13 concussions while in XPW, that Black's motto to the locker room before shows was "Be stiff and juice hard," and that doctors would be backstage at XPW shows to stitch people up on the spot.

The second death match tournament was also the night of Supreme's second worst injury (behind the fire incident), according to his 2012 In Your Head interview. He cracked his ribs after botching a jump off a ladder and landing chest-first on the ring apron. Asked about the third KOTDM tournament in 2002, Supreme mentioned in the same interview about how challenging it was for that tournament to top the previous two. Supreme was Luke's first real involvement in the death match world, wrestling Luke in the second round of the 2002 tournament after Luke's tame first round match vs. Massaro. According to Luke's interview with Sam Roberts, his trainer Grimes was "furious" that XPW management contacted Luke directly about being in the death match tournament without asking his trainer first if he was ready.

Luke recalled to me that Black wanted him to do what Luke thought were some unsafe stunts, including a shooting star press off of a scaffold at Fallout, which he refused to do. He also recalled on Xtreme Memories that "I had to pay this 'price' to show how tough I was because I put my hand up for a chairshot." That "price," Luke said, involved what he considered to be a form of retaliation from Black - having to be "crucified" in order to have his arms pinned so he couldn't put his hands up again to block chairshots, resulting in a "a bad concussion [that] really did some damage...long-term." Luke told me that Supreme didn't want to do the crucified chairshots, but was told he'd be fired if he didn't.

Luke also said on Xtreme Memories that " hitting so hard from the 450°'' splash off the balcony resulted in thumbtacks having to be pulled "out [of his hands] with pliers because they couldn't be picked out. I couldn't close my hands for like two weeks...I couldn't pick up my kid for like two weeks." Luke seemed to agree with what Grimes told Angel about the fans not being there for you in those moments, saying "That's the side that people don't see," and even added a criticism of Black, saying he "just didn't care about" Luke's injuries having to get dealt with via pliers.

Not all of the XPW death match wrestlers were crazy about bloodletting. Messiah has gone on record in interviews saying that he isn't a huge fan of bleeding, as some might think, and that he enjoys straight wrestling, calling it "a double-edged sword." He has repeatedly told the story of just showing up to the Extreme Associates office one day in early 2000, seeing a dry erase board with a sign up list, and deciding to enroll as a participant to be able to say he did a death match once. However, he, in his words in an Ultraviolent Radio interview on February 23, 2011, "was too good for [his] own good" like Luke was and as a result, sometimes got pigeonholed into death matches. "I didn't want to be a death match wrestler," Messiah said on the podcast. "I did it because I knew I was good at it."

Luke had a similar view, having said in interviews that even though he never liked doing death matches, he turned out to be good at them, and Supreme ended up pitching the idea of putting the KOTDM Title on him, which happened at Fallout. Meanwhile, Webb also said in the *Daily Bruin* in 2001 "I don't enjoy getting cut up, but it comes with the territory." Darlin, Webb's valet, told me in 2020 "I wish the wrestlers got paid more for what they did. I always felt they were underpaid for all they put their bodies through."

GQ Money had interesting comments on the subject of whether danger was par for the course, though, saying on the May 18, 2008 False Count Radio podcast that "every crazy thing I did I did very safely, so I never injured myself my entire time in XPW. I rarely woke up sore the day after matches, and I maintained a very, very healthy mind, body, and spirit throughout all of my matches."

Grimes even took limited precautions for the Free Fall bump, considering ahead of time whether he wanted to go off "straight" at a perpendicular angle or at a diagonal angle. Due to the sudden nature of the throw, he ultimately went diagonally off, whereas Angel went more perpendicularly. Grimes indicated on Awesome Fight Bomb Radio that after he ricocheted off the ropes, he "knew to tuck…[his] left shoulder, and [his] chin and turn inward" to his left after sensing that he was headed toward "the turnbuckle area." If he hadn't done that and thereby successfully shifted his weight in mid-air, he would have "flipped out onto the floor and probably broke my neck." Instead, he bounced back into the ring and landed safely. So, while the actual dive from the scaffold wasn't "a controlled bump" in Black's words, Grimes' performer instincts took over and he adjusted his weight in a split second so as to land as safely as possible from this extremely risky stunt. Grimes walked backstage on his own two feet after the fans had left the building.

Granted, not everyone (namely Supreme) was as lucky as GQ, Angel, and Grimes to emerge from XPW "injury-free"(in GQ's words), However, on a positive note, there are, according to GQ and to a degree Grimes as well, generally safety measures that can be taken when performing dangerous stunts.

9. Gimmicks, Booking, & Storyline Delivery

XPW had its fair share of characters and storylines that were controversial and outrageous. Sabu wrote in his 2019 autobiography that XPW storylines were "weird, and that was coming from me, who up until this point thought I had seen everything wrestling had to offer." Messiah also had a negative view of the storylines in his SMV interview, saying "[The TV show] was just garbage. We were doing jokes, but only we got the jokes. The viewing public had no idea what was funny about it. Only we thought it was funny."

Angel must never have heard that Messiah interview because he said in an January 20, 2010 Awesome Bomb Fight Radio interview that "Whether you liked the XPW live shows or not, the TV shows nobody's ever talked crap on. They've always loved the TV shows. They were funny. They were entertaining." Like Angel, Kleinrock, not surprisingly, painted the eccentricities in a more positive manner also, going so far as to tell Joe Feeney on the *Creative Control* podcast in November 2014, "I defy you to find another indie...that had such character development, such storyline, such actual following through of those storylines, such continuity of those storylines." Kleinrock went so far as to say on Xtreme Memories that "You could not find plot holes and loopholes in our show from week to week to week."

There was a five month gap in live events after July 2000's Go Funk Yourself, and Kleinrock explained on Xtreme Memories that "You saw what our actual...abilities were when we went all those months with no wrestling, but we still made this entertaining TV show that people were watching because it had the skits and the vignettes and the different packages." Indeed, some of the more memorable segments and storylines of XPW TV came during that nearly half a year gap in live shows, including TOOL and Luis Cypher's terrorization of Webb and Darlin, Negro Claus, Homeless Jimmy's life story, and Rocco and Jocko's adventures.

One of the most talked about gimmicks in XPW was that of Messiah. He was originally supposed to be "Luke," half of a "brothers" tag team of The Moral Crusaders with Matthew, but the person pegged for Matthew suddenly disappeared. So, Messiah asked to do the gimmick as a singles wrestler, which Black was initially hesitant about, but Supreme encouraged him. Messiah was even going to be "Jesus" around the same time, but he didn't want to be called that. Ring announcer Mark "Guido" Mancini actually announced him as "Jesus" during his debut and he got mad. He was given the choice of "Savior" or "Messiah" and the Messiah name stuck.

Of course, Messiah's character was later recycled for Altar Boy Luke, and Luke's partner, Altar Boy Matthew, has long been a source of questions from XPW fans. Matthew made one appearance in XPW at Liberty or Death and then disappeared. He had just moved to California and wanted to get into the company, and kept pestering GQ about submitting a tape. Finally, he came to the office and gave a tape to Byron, but it got lost. So, he brought another tape to GQ, who remembers it vividly:

"His highlight video was all in-ring stuff, in front of some good crowds, too...He was great! So, we brought him in to tryout in person, and he went balls out with some big dives and shit, but he was pretty rusty on his basics, and also at bumping. We told him we liked him, but wanted him to train a bit with us before we would do anything. Around the same time, I had gotten Luke's tape from Vic. We were scheduling the tag team tournament, and we knew we had these 2 kids, both real skinny and kind of lanky. So Rob was like, 'Let's make them The Altar Boys.' Matt wasn't really ready, but in a tag team match, we were able to hide his weaknesses, and let him hit his high spots, and people loved them both because they were good. The biggest problem was, he would get concussions, or bang his head when he bumped, so he was real injury prone.
It gets interesting.

"At that show, LOD, he was so excited to be there. We needed someone to go pick someone else up from the airport, and he said it was OK to let someone use his car. Whoever was driving totaled his car! And he was planning on driving back to Iowa, where he was from, the next day. So he was so upset, and worried, and pissed, but he was the nicest kid in the world, so he didn't show any of his anger...he was just distraught that he wasn't going to be able to get home, or get his stuff home. That's where the benevolence and good side of Rob Black comes in. Rob flew him home and shipped all of his stuff back to Iowa. And that was kind of the end...I just remember how happy he was to be on the show...and how proud I was of both him and Luke, who were both guys I really pulled for. And that's the story of Altar Boy Matthew."

There were plans to bring Matthew back from Iowa, but they never materialized.

Meanwhile, Exodus, the giant who made a single appearance, attacking Messiah at the end of The Night XPW Stood Still, was a friend of GQ who worked as Extreme Associates' receptionist. "It was leading to him vs. Messiah, but [Exodus] got impatient and took off," GQ explains.

Crimson, another giant who would appear a few times, was played by So-Cal indie wrestler Matt Sinister. GQ recalls that originally the plan was for Crimson to be Veronica's Caine's brother. Black talked about Crimson on an April 1, 2020 "Rob Black Show":

"It was a good gimmick. We just executed it wrong...He had a mask, a white mask, and the premise was he would bust guys open, take their blood, and then smear it on his mask, so he was a collector of people's blood, until his mask was a crimson mask of blood."

Meanwhile, the "Mr. 80s" gimmick that eventually went to Dynamite D was originally going to be crossed with the Cybil character (Slammers' Jesse Balin). As McMillan told me years later, "Cybil could not pull [the 'Mr. '80s' gimmick] off and the [Cybil] gimmick was phasing out," so McMillan took it over. Black confirmed that Cybil was supposed to involve aspects of the "Mr. '80s" gimmick in a June 30, 1999 interview with Gene Ross, saying:

"Cybil's not real sure who he is. He comes out in a dress and plays with a doll. He's got multi-personalities, and the personalities are all wrestlers. Some nights. he thinks he's Hulk Hogan. Some nights, he thinks he's Randy Savage."

Several XPW gimmicks were influenced by films, pop culture, and history. S&M character TOOL, who Kloss said on a mid-2000s In Your Head interview built the XPW TV set, was inspired by the Nicholas Cage movie *8mm*. Meanwhile, Carlito Montana developed from Al Pacino in *Scarface* and Pogo The Clown, of course, was inspired by child murderer John Wayne Gacy and Black's interest in serial killers. Kleinrock has said in interviews that the backstory of the Homeless Jimmy character was inspired in part by not only Hollywood movie *Chasing Amy*, but also by psychologist Abraham Maslow's hierarchy of needs theory. He stated on "Xtreme Memories" that Jimmy's character evolved from Maslow's idea that "if you don't have food and shelter and you don't have this and you don't have that, then you can never have love, and you can never get to self-actualization because you need the basics to survive."

There was a story behind even the patently ridiculous characters. For instance, Colorado indie wrestler Jenocide, a friend of GQ from his CWO promotion back home, dressed as a monkey at Free Fall against Rizzono. A few months later, Jenocide became Raphael Mohammed of The Black Panthers, but the transition from one character to another didn't end up being explained like the original plan called for. GQ explained in September 2003:

"We were thinking of calling them The Black Gorillas or something like that. Essentially [Mohammed] did that match. Then in a future show there would be two monkeys. Then finally like three, when they would take off the suits and proclaim that the whole monkey suit was some racist shit set up by the man, and then start a reign of militant black terror - three big, bad, black men with attitudes…Mohammed, [Salid] Jihad, [K. Malik] Shebazz."

So-Cal indie wrestler Big Babi Slymm portrayed Jihad. Shebazz, meanwhile, was played by Ron Killings, who said in an August 2005 "In Your Head" interview that he "hated" his XPW name. He told me in 2006 that he has a great affinity for Kleinrock, and that there were plans (which never came to fruition) to move him away from The Black Panthers so that he became more of a singles wrestler.

In addition to Jenocide, GQ was also responsible for bringing Smokey Carmichael, his Colorado tag team partner, in for a one-night (Hostile Takeover) alternate Black Panthers pairing with Brian (Malcolm) XL, saying "I actually told Rob that I would sacrifice my pay for that show to bring him and Luke to Philly." GQ said that XL was a last-minute replacement after Killings had "some family problems come up that night before," although Killing insisted to me that he was never booked for Hostile Takeover.

A character that had a lot more long-term success in XPW than the Panthers was Shark Boy. The night of his debut, he was the most over talent on the show, as the fans chanted "We want Shark Boy!" even when he wasn't in the ring. Shark Boy told me:

"[XPW] always seemed to have a really creative direction to go with my character, and after years of hearing from WWE and everyone else that, 'Oh, well, we just can't come up with anything creative, can't come up with anything,' it's like 'Here's this company that wrestling's almost an afterthought. The forethought is the girls and the hardcore and wrestling's almost an afterthought, and *yet* they kinda got it right for awhile, you know?' And they let me do my thing, and it was just really a lot of fun, and I connected with the crowd like I haven't done in many places I've worked."

Some potentially controversial gimmicks never saw the light of day in XPW. For instance, according to Messiah's April 2018 interview with Cory Kastle, a character called "Mr. Fister" (whose finisher would be an ass punch) was discussed.

Black had also come up with the idea for "Percy Fabulous," which Dynamite D was pegged as at one point. McMillan explained Percy as "an over the top gay wrestler who was just Fabulous with a high pitched voice similar to Chris Tucker in *Fifth Element*." Conversely, Black's account of the character in a June 30, 1999 interview with Gene Ross indicated that someone black would portray him, saying Percy would be a "flamboyant black homosexual" who managed The Westside NGZ.

In that interview, Black also talked about his intention to showcase "Mr. I.M. Dreadful, Ian Michael Dreadful. Basically he's 6'8, 300 pounds. He's not bad, he's not cool, he's not incredible, just dreadful. He comes out with two henchman-type guys. He's very mysterious."

There was also the idea for "Rudolph Heimlich" before XPW even launched. Black told Ross that Heimlich was to be "a rascist, nazi-guy...He hates blacks, Jews, Italians. He hates everybody. He's an equal opportunity hater and he's managed by Little Adolph."

In the early 2000s interview with Roger T. Pipe, Black mentioned plans for a racial Palestinian gimmick. When asked about it a couple years later, GQ said Juantastico was to be involved and was "growing his beard" out, but the angle was "scrapped" as "bad taste" after the September 11 attacks. GQ explained that "They were going to come to the ring throwing rocks and all that, and they would have been known as 'The P.L.O.'" Juantastico admitted on Xtreme Memories that his own willingness to do the gimmick somewhat soured after 9/11, too. Similarly, after 9/11, Black wanted to do a segment where the EA secretary would end up covered in what was supposed to look like anthrax, but he was talked out of it.

One gimmick for a somewhat intolerant character did come to partial fruition - "Luis Cypher," who was played by Jessica Darlin's real-life husband, Bobby and on-screen, portrayed TOOL's handler. Originally, Cypher didn't like his wife's wrestling involvement, even telling Ross in a February 2001 interview, "My wife got in XPW first and I prayed every single day that wrestling would go away. I wanted nothing to do with goddamn wrestling because I was envious and jealous of watching my wife walk out with wrestlers." In time, though, when he got recruited to XPW, this controversial role grew on him and he ended up having "fun" playing "the bad guy."

Cypher explained that his character was intended to blur the line. Fans were supposed to not be able to decipher "whether that character's me or not" and not "know if" he is "a Nazi" who will "sympathize with racism." However, Cypher indicated that he wanted to convey to fans that he was invested in "every inch of that character." He boasted that because "there's never been a white, racial character in wrestling," his character was "the most hated man in the history of wrestling soon-to-come." On Xtreme Memories,

Kleinrock pointed out the irony "that here's this Jewish kid [Kleinrock] writing these outlandish promos for [Cypher], but I was writing using history books, and using real quotes, and real philosophies."

As for future plans for the character, Cypher told Ross, "I've got a good feeling that Rob's going to let me go with this" character and predicted that "if he does, [you had] better watch out. It's going to be unsafe to be at an XPW event with me there because it just so happens I'm going to have some supporters show up, too." Darlin says, however, that she "never" feared for her husband's safety "because all wrestlers knew about his character and if anything ever came of it, they'd all have his back. They were like family."

Besides Cypher, Kleinrock also was partly responsible for Devon "Crowbar" Storm's XPW characters, which Storm described to me in 2006 as "dark", "evil," and "gothic." Storm's "Judas" alias in XPW was short-lived because he, being religious and thinking it was too close to "Jesus," requested it be changed. Storm then became "Salem" and told WrestlingFever.de that he "loved playing" that character because it provided "creative freedom to lay out my matches and interviews and vignettes the way I wanted to."

Storm told me he was supposed to lead a "cult" that would also include "converts" Chris Hero, Super Crazy, Malice, and Altar Boy Luke, but it never panned out. Hero, who praised XPW in his 2003 Smart Mark Video (SMV) "Best on the Indies" shoot interview, mentioned in a January 2018 tweet that Jim Mitchell was supposed to lead the (in his words) "New Church-esque faction." The partnership between Luke and Salem did briefly see the light of day, as they aligned with each other and shot some backstage vignettes in early 2003 and were both aligned against Grimes in Pittsburgh.

Doomhammer was another character that never fully materialized, other than a few vignettes that aired on XPW TV. In September 2003, GQ recalled plans for Doomhammer:

"We all (Rob, Kevin, me, and Webb) thought that was hysterical, and we were inspired by the old Glacier hype from back in the day (in WCW). The idea was to hype him up for a long time with the promos, and then have him debut in this big, robotic, Robocop-like outfit. And when Shane was doing promos in the office as owner, you'd hear the mechanical Doomhammer walking by, and then like see his big robotic arms or something, with Shane yelling at him to take off that ridiculous costume. It was going to be a spoof, and it would have been very funny."

Several people were to credit for the delivery of XPW storylines and the production of the TV shows. Of course, there were the commentators, Kloss and Rivera. Kloss reminisced on a mid-2000s In Your Head podcast that "There was a chemistry there in the broadcast booth that I think we really hit on and audiences responded to it, too." Rivera recalls that Black and Kleinrock would have "a loose script" in the form of "sheets of paper with bullet points" ready for Kloss and Rivera each Wednesday night, which was when they would typically record voiceovers. Black and Kleinrock would tell the commentators to do what they wanted, as long as they hit the bullet points. "Typically it would take about three or four takes" to get the best one, Rivera recalls. Kloss described XPW TV on back to back "Xtreme Memories" episodes in August 2020 with GQ Money and Kaos as having "a lot of thought and care and strategy that went into it," mentioning that "it was like a science class, the way the chalkboard was laid out of what was gonna transpire just for that one television episode." Rivera remembers Pogo having specific ideas and suggestions for the commentators to say.

Lazie also had a role in the creative aspect, especially as it related to Sabu's storylines. Sabu's debut, with him sneaking up behind Douglas and Candido, as well as Douglas' debut, with the lights coming back on to reveal him and his subsequent promo, were all his and Douglas' ideas. Lazie adds in 2020 that "I was involved with [storylines of] all the outside talent and some of the homegrown talent." He says he helped develop the ideas for the King of the Death Match belt and tournament. He suggested to Black that the death match tournament trophy be called the "Bruiser Brody Cup," but Black asked "Who's Bruiser Brody?" Lazie remembers 20 years later, "Those guys [in management] didn't even know about 'death match' before I got there. I showed Rob and Kevin a video called 'Those Bloody, Bloody Matches' which I got about 10 years prior from [Rivera]."

Starting in mid-to-late 2001, GQ Money would play an important role in some of the controversial gimmicks. He reminisces:

"Rob and myself came up with crazy things, and Kevin was the little angel on the shoulder saying, 'You can't do that. That's in bad taste even for us.' That's why I got along so well with Rob for a while. We both liked pushing buttons, and doing crazy shit. We realized that our target audience wasn't little kids, and we felt the adult based product with serious issues was much more entertaining. And we both felt, 'Hey, this is wrestling. We can do anything we want.'"

Webb played a creative role, and not only in his own character's storylines. Webb said in an April 2008 Rubber Guard Radio interview that he "stole the [Homeless] Jimmy gimmick from the commissioner of Extremely Strange Wrestling." Lazie, meanwhile, said that Webb had many great booking ideas and that he would walk into a room, shout a tremendous idea, and then walk out, while Rivera said that Webb would write funny lines on paper and feed them to him. Steele went so far as to say that Webb, Kleinrock, and Black were XPW's main clique.

Webb also was vital to the TV production aspect, recalling in an April 2008 Rubber Guard Radio interview that the early 2000s would involve him "spending half the day editing porn and the other half of the day working on the XPW show." GQ told me in September 2003:

"Webb was very busy at XPW. He edited all the time, like all day and all night. He got frustrated...In all honesty, Webb was the backbone of XPW. When he left, things went to shit...Production values dropped dramatically when he left, and I had no interest in even trying to step in for him."

Kloss said the same thing on the Mike Hartsfield Xtreme Memories edition about the TV show edit quality deteriorating when Webb left.

Veronica emphasized in her March 2003 XMR interview that "Webb basically was their whole TV show, their entire home video…The cool music videos that you've seen or whatever. He did all that, and there's just nobody that they have [that] works over there that is as talented - anywhere near as talented - and that would work for what they were asking him to work for." However, with his knee injury and surgery and the XPW office going through changes, as well as problems developing between him and Black (according to my 2004 interview with him), things didn't end in an ideal way. Webb told me that the New Year's Revolution 3 double-shot in January 2003 was his last show.

Meanwhile, Kleinrock, one of the people (along with Byron) who took over most of the TV production when Webb left, received praise from Grimes, who said "he was the thinker, the smart one, the brains behind the operation." Like Jimmy said on The Death Hour podcast in January 2020, Grimes believes that if Kleinrock had a bigger role in XPW, the promotion would've been more successful. Meanwhile, Rivera told me in May 2020 that Kleinrock was "the conduit, the lifeline" that held XPW together and that his strength was "being able to corral all of these dudes and all of these ideas into one coherent package to present each week on TV." Kloss agreed, telling me Kleinrock "made the wheels go around," and Kraq mentioned Kleinrock's interpersonal skills, saying "Kevin knew how to talk to you. He knew how to get you engaged." Phenomenal Phil said on an April 2, 2021 WrestleBoss podcast, "He was the person who Rob could always count on to get things done." Konnan praised Kleinrock as well, saying he was "very approachable, very easy to talk to…This business and world needs more guys like Kevin."

Lazie, meanwhile, says that Kleinrock knows wrestling, so he has potential to be a good promoter; however, he was, in Lazie's words, Black's "yes-man" and he "lacks the backbone" to stand up for what he believes in. Lazie said that Black essentially passed Kleinrock's ideas off as his own, mentioning that Kleinrock would say, "Rob, I got this great idea" and would explain it. Black would say he wasn't interested in it, but a few minutes later, would call Kleinrock back, Lazie said, and say "Hey, I got this idea" and explain Kleinrock's same idea. Rizzono concurred, calling Kleinrock Black's "gopher" and "boy toy" who was attached to Black's hip and followed him around, though he admitted that Kleinrock worked very hard. Messiah commented on Kleinrock's relationship with Black on Xtreme Memories saying, "Kevin took a lot of crap from Rob that was Rob's fault. Kevin took a lot of cannon fodder because of Rob's BS and because Rob didn't want to deal with consequences on stuff that he had put in motion."

Kleinrock has always said others deserve credit in addition to him for XPW's creative affairs. He said on the August 9, 2019 "Vegas BadBoyz" podcast that "There were certain people that I wrote for, certain people [Rob] wrote for, certain people that could just do their own thing, specifically naming Webb and Steele as the latter." Kleinrock said on Xtreme Memories that for those "clearly defined characters" who had trouble finding "their unique voices…I had to try to speak as that character. I'd be driving my car, speaking out loud promos as these guys, as I was trying to figure out what to write for them." He added that "the undercard fell to me...That was what I was good at, was writing the rest of the stories, filling in the plot holes, and making sure that we had consistent storytelling, and a lot of the time that means booking backwards - where are we trying to get to? What are we gonna do to get there?"

Black, of course, had the final say on everything. Kloss said on the August 15, 2020 "Xtreme Memories" episode that Black brought "realism" to the XPW product and GQ added that Black's involvement and "his crazy outlandishness" and "magnetic charisma...made things matter." Grimes says that Black's strength was also his weakness - while he was willing to try anything, "he didn't always think before he tried." Lazie, meanwhile, said that Black "knows how to entertain," but his weakness was that he spent money in the wrong places--for example, paying Douglas to be a consultant was dumb, Lazie says, and "he spent money as a mark."

Kleinrock defended Black, though, saying on Xtreme Memories that "Rob does not get nearly the credit that he deserves for what he contributed on the creative level to XPW," and Kloss immediately agreed. Kloss said on Barbwire-Press.com's *Deep Impact* show that "Rob really had a lot of wrestling knowledge that people really don't give him credit for." Meanwhile, on the August 9, 2019 *Vegas BadBoyz* podcast, Kleinrock credited Black for Pogo's character and angles and has said in interviews that Black always wrote the main event storylines. Kaos also said on Xtreme Memories that Black deserves more credit than he gets for using name talent strategically to elevate local talent, and Kloss told me that Black's strengths were that he never held back and that he typically gave the fans what they wanted.

So several people, including Kloss, Rivera, Lazie, GQ, Webb, Kleinrock, and Black, were part of the creative and production process, from vocalizing ideas to putting storylines to paper to making sure they came out well on tape. XPW storylines were a team effort in every respect, and it's not a surprise that, given more than half of those aforementioned people also worked for the porn side of things, the porn company's controversial nature rubbed off onto the wrestling storylines.

With most talent, the controversial angles were acceptable; for instance, both Angel and Kraq said on Xtreme Memories and Kraq emphasized to me that they were taught early on in wrestling not to question what storylines they were given and to take what opportunities they got, and they applied that mindset to their roles in XPW. Kloss went so far as to say on Messiah's Xtreme Memories edition that "'Pushing the envelope' is a mild description of what we did." and that "bulldoze the envelope" is a more appropriate term for what they did. Black wasn't exaggerating when he said to Luke Y. Thompson in *The LA New Times* in 2000, saying "If we can't get arrested for it, we'll do it," as XPW featured storylines ranging from religion to racism to, on one 1999 show, rape. Angel went so far as to say on Xtreme Memories that "There was no limit to what Rob's and XPW's imagination was," and he was right.

5. Extreme Invasions

XPW was the place to be when ECW started developing money problems, and especially after it folded. Even managers like "Judge" Jeff Jones and referees such as John "Pee Wee" Moore flocked to the company for appearances. Kleinrock went so far as to tell Joe Feeney in November 2014 on the Creative Control podcast, "It pretty much became well known in ECW that if you got fired or if you quit, there was definitely at least one or two paydays in XPW [waiting for you]." He elaborated on Xtreme Memories, saying "Any time anybody left ECW, we were the first phone call they make. People think that it was us recruiting. At first, of course, [yes]...but people would be calling us."

John Kronus was the ECW wrestler who lasted longest in XPW, and there are plenty of noteworthy anecdotes about him. Josh Lazie recalls that one night after a show, a wrestler had brought a woman back to the Bakersfield hotel and went around asking if anyone had condoms. When he arrived at Kronus, the former-Eliminator responded that he did have a condom, but that after what he did with it in a shower earlier that day, he didn't think that this particular wrestler would want to use it. Suffice to say, the wrestler in question continued on to another person. Also, Kronus had abnormal sleeping hours and would rarely bring soap, conditioner, or shampoo. As a result, he'd sometimes bang on wrestlers' hotel room doors in the wee hours of the morning asking to borrow these bathing products.

Kronus and Steve Rizzono sometimes made early morning trips to the bank to cash their checks, during which he talked about his son constantly. One morning, Kronus was standing in Western Union with Rizzono, wearing pajamas, a tank top, Rizzono's hat, and no shoes as he wrote a telegram to his son, accompanied by a check for a toy his son wanted for his birthday. The thought that he couldn't give his son this gift in person (since he was on the road) upset Kronus, and the best he could do was send money for it. At the same time, he also wrote to his wife a check designated towards their mortgage. When Kronus messed up writing one of the checks, he shouted "FAAACK!" at the top of his lungs. Other confused customers turned their heads toward him. That morning, Kronus sent home to New England one envelope for his wife with mortgage money and a separate telegram featuring a check for the toy and a loving letter to his son. Rizzono says that it was impossible to be depressed around Kronus, who he said wanted to move to California.

Another time, Kronus was riding with Kris Kloss on U.S. Route (Highway) 101. Kloss wouldn't allow him to smoke a cigarette in his car, so the mammoth Kronus started pleading with Kloss, while literally huddling down on his knees below the dashboard like a toddler: "Pwease pwease pwease pwease pweeeaaase???!!!" Finally, Kronus asked Kloss whether he could smoke if he opened the window. Kloss was agreeable. Instead of doing what Kloss expected and simply opening the window and smoking from inside, Kronus proceeded to hang nearly his entire 300 pound body out the window of a speeding car just so that he could smoke without disrespecting Kloss' wishes. At one point, Kronus stuck his head back into the car and shouted, "How's dat, Kwoss? You ain't gettin' any smoke in der, ah ya? Cause if you ah, I wiw thwow dis puppy out!" To cap it all off, while he was nearly falling out the window of this fast-moving vehicle, Kronus realized the road was lined with cactuses. Kronus began "marking out" and begging Kloss to stop the car so that he could get a better look: "Hey Kwoss, dose wook wike dose cactuses I saw in dose Speedy Gonzawez cawtoons!"

In addition to smoking, Kronus also drank alcohol. Grimes mentioned hiding under the ring with Kronus before the Rapture show and staying there for two hours until their cue to come out and mount a Black Army attack. Kronus brought a beer cooler and drank about 12 beers while under the ring. When he had to go to the bathroom, Kronus urinated into a nearby bucket. Kikuzawa recounted a similar story from January 2001 when he and Nosawa were scheduled for a match that also included Kronus and Jimmy. When Kronus finally arrived from a late flight, he had a big vodka bottle that was already half done. Before they went to the ring to wrestle, Kikuzawa said to Kronus, "It already half gone. I see your bottle half full." Then Kronus took the bottle out of his pocket and showed Kikuzawa that it was empty by that point. Kronus said, "Tonight, we do blood party." Kikuzawa remembers that all four bled that night.

Kronus would also take showers in the women's locker room and freak the porn stars out by leaving blood trails. Kristi Myst told

RF Video that Kronus would frequently hit on her. He sometimes left blood on his face hours after his match. One time, according to ref Danny Ramirez, Kronus walked up to media reporters wearing a crimson mask, wiped the blood off his face so that it landed on the floor right in front of their feet, and walked off without saying a word. Webb recalled on Rubber Guard Radio in April 2008 that Kronus was "the nicest guy in the world." but that "before he gets in the shower, he's probably gonna strip naked, and he's probably gonna shake his body like a dog, and he's gonna spray blood all over the walls. You know what I mean? Nice guy, though. But, you know, he's probably gonna get you in a little bit of trouble with the venues."

Steele shared a similar story, saying that he was returning to the main wrestlers' locker room one night when Kronus called him over to a small electrical closet that he had apparently converted into his own private dressing room. Kronus was nude and said "Look, there's blood on my weiner!" Steele didn't want to see that, but recalled "He looked so happy when he said it. He was very child-like."

Interestingly enough, there is more footage of Kronus wearing XPW logo t-shirts at indie shows from 1999 to 2002 (including at a CZW show before the war with XPW) than not wearing XPW t-shirts during that era.

The Pitbulls, meanwhile, did about five XPW shows in 1999. They were the only two people to wrestle for ECW, then XPW, and later ECW again. Asked about his experience 20 years later in December 2019, Gary Wolf (the only surviving member of the tag team) said that Big Dick Dudley got them into the company. Wolf treated XPW like a vacation, looking at it as "a gig at Paramount in Hollywood for a weekend" with theme parks and more. He was disappointed that at the last minute Black cancelled a show the last Sunday of November, as they were out in California already for the Saturday event. However, some porn girls brought his partner Anthony Durante back to the hotel that night and Wolf headed over to the Playboy Mansion with them and partied. Also while in California for XPW, Wolf and Durante together went to an MTV after-party celebration at Universal Studios, where they saw Ron Jeremy with about five women in tow.

Wolf also recalled some funny stories, including how for one appearance, he and Durante weren't aware until the last moment that they were supposed to enter through the front door and not the entrance curtain, so they ended up running out on Hollywood Boulevard to the front of the venue with their dog collars, chains, and spikes and thought they would be arrested. Additionally, Wolf reminisces that during a brawl, he and Rocco Rock knocked over a giant metal "X" that Black had just purchased and he came through the curtain flying off the handle.

Wolf mentions that the only problems he had in XPW were the day of The Pitbulls' steel cage match against The Westsiders. Black gave them a move-for-move script of how he wanted the match to go. Wolf told Black that he and Durante were professionals and that if he had something he wanted them to get across in the match, they would certainly convey it, but writing things out wasn't how it worked. That same night, Wolf asked one of his opponents if he knew how to safely but realistically ram his head into the steel, only to realize that neither Westsider had been in a cage match before. Wolf emphasizes that he didn't mind working with the Westsiders, but just thought that Black pushed his wrestlers too fast, causing some communication problems.

Axl Rotten also did a few shows for XPW, shortly after The Pitbulls. In an interview with John Mikels in 2005, he summarized XPW as having "had all the right ideas, just all the wrong people." Alternatively, he called XPW "the drizzling shits" to RF Video. On In Your Head Radio in 2006, Axl mentioned that he "hung out with Ron Jeremy" and the porn stars. He elaborated on the partying atmosphere of XPW in his RF shoot, saying "You get out there in California. You're fuckin' around with porn stars you're doing drugs. It was a vacation. You fuckin' drive down to Mexico and go to the pharmacy." When asked what the craziest thing he saw in XPW was, he said "I was probably involved in it. There [were] porn stars and cocaine. You put one and two together."

Both Rotten "brothers," Ian included, had negative comments on their XPW rival Supreme in their RF shoots, with Axl saying Supreme "was afraid of me the first time we ever wrestled" and Ian saying that "I don't think Supreme's in that upper echelon" of death match wrestlers. Webb said on Rubber Guard Radio in April 2008 that "to ensure that no indie guy that he didn't know" would "stiff him or whatever, [Axl] made sure to let Supreme know that he kept a knife in his boot."

Axl and Ian's ally during ECW's early days, Terry Funk, wrestled for XPW three times. One appearance, Liberty or Death, was a day before Funk's birthday, so XPW got him a birthday cake to celebrate backstage. At that show, Funk saw GQ shoot segments backstage and, amazed by his camera talent, wrote in his autobiography that "Vince should look this guy up and hire him!" without mentioning GQ's name.

Funk's ECW opponent Chris Candido, along with his valet Tammy Lynn Sytch, had two runs in XPW, one in 2000 and another in 2002 and 2003. They were in WCW at the same time as their first XPW tenure. In the course of a period from March 25 to April 16, Candido wrestled about four times for WCW and three times for XPW, competing for XPW in the weeks between his WCW matches, including wrestling one time for each company in a 24 hour period. Damien Steele said that Candido worked the hardest in-ring of the name talents who he wrestled in XPW. Messiah said on Cory Kastle's podcast in April 2018 that XPW stopped using Candido the first time because he no-showed some events. During their second run, there was talk of pairing them with Angel for an angle based off of Anna Nicole Smith. Candido and Tammy were all for the proposed angle, which never happened.

Candido had a drug problem while in XPW. Douglas recalls one time in XPW that he saw Candido and [Axl Rotten] sticking themselves with needles. [I don't know] whether it was steroids or if it was drugs or what it was. I yanked them both by their arms into the bathrooms and read them the riot act and basically told them they would be fired if they did it again." Douglas claims, "That was the only time I ever saw Chris doing that."

There are three humorous stories about Candido from XPW. During one night of the D-Day triple-shot in May 2000, Candido had rubbed "hot stuff," a substance wrestlers use to make their muscles look shiny, all over his body. One is supposed to wash their hands immediately after rubbing it on them and never let it make contact with their face. Candido accidentally touched his penis, so his groin felt like it was on fire. He started moaning and ran into the shower Rizzono (who said there were plans for a Candido vs. Abdullah The Butcher program in XPW) was just using and rinsed his penis, before telling Rizzono, "Yeah, us wrestlers, we aren't very bright."

At the tail-end of the same weekend's tour, Candido wrestled Messiah. Candido called their match back to Black before it happened. As Messiah explained on Yakuza Kick Radio in September 2013, "Chris, when he got excited--he would stutter and he would talk like a mile a minute." Black nodded along, but when Candido walked away, asked Messiah "Did you understand a friggin' word that guy just said?"

Shark Boy, meanwhile, told me a funny story from the January 18, 2003 Q&A session, at which he sat next to Candido:

"[In response to a fan question] Candido said 'Well, you know, it's a funny business, this business. It's the difference between me working on television for WWE or sitting up here in the ring next to Shark Boy.' It was kind of an off-handed insult, but at the same time I loved Chris so much that it's actually one of the fonder memories I have, is him kind of ribbing me in front of everybody like that."

Candido told RF that he enjoyed his first XPW stay in 2000, but that during his second run, his local bank manager was doing him favors and trying to make his bouncing XPW checks go through even though they kept getting rejected as "insufficient funds." He was arrested by a Manasquan, NJ police detective for grand larceny because he appeared to be "kiting checks" (a form of "check fraud"). To get out of the predicament, Candido had to pay the bank back about $10,000, which XPW never reimbursed him

Like Candido, Chris Hamrick was also still part of XPW when it folded. Hamrick has always praised XPW in interviews consistently more than any other former-ECW talent. Hamrick was brought into XPW due to New Jack's recommendation and in turn ended up developing some talent scout leverage in XPW.

For instance, at Kleinrock's request, Hamrick called The S.A.T (Jose & Joel Maximo) about wrestling Mexico's Most

Wanted at Hostile Takeover. Hamrick says they twice told him they wanted to do the show before he read they were doing another show. "They never even called me to tell me they changed their minds," Hamrick explained to me in May 2003. "They told me later that they were afraid [their trainer] Mikey Whipwreck would get mad at them."

Hamrick was directly involved in his own controversy during the Philly run. He had been paired with Tracy Smothers in a tag team called "Southern Comfort," after a similar idea for a confederate tag team of Hamrick and Webb had been toyed with. In a match, Southern Comfort tried to attack "The Hardcore Homo" Angel with a cutting utensil. Online, they got criticism for disrespecting Messiah, whose thumb had been cut off with gardening shears in real life. Hamrick told me:

"It had nothing at all to do with the Messiah incident. Think about it. If a homo came across two rednecks and started fighting with them, more than likely they are going to cut his ding ding off. Well, that was the point we were trying to get across and since we couldn't use fingernail clippers, we had to use something everyone could see. Shane [Douglas] suggested scissors. I suggested garden shears. Sorry, but I do not think about the Messiah incident 24/7. So, when I suggested them, I didn't think about that."

Kleinrock told Hamrick that XPW was going to put the tag team titles on Southern Comfort on the April 19, 2003 Pittsburgh show, but the show never ended up happening. Smothers, meanwhile, had two runs in XPW, one in 2000 and also the one during its dying days. Smothers said in his Highspots shoot interview that Sabu and Douglas got him booked for his first XPW tenure. Steele mentions that Smothers voiced his opinion that Steele and Rizzono should be a tag team, although it never happened. In a WrestleWarehouse.com shoot interview in the late 2000s, over five years after his second XPW run, Smothers remembered the real name of Kaos, his Go Funk Yourself opponent who told me that

Smothers was the XPW veteran who he learned the most from due to them calling their match entirely on the fly.

Smothers described himself to WrestleWarehouse.com as having been a "trainer" and "agent" in XPW. The trainer part has to do with him holding pre-show workouts for the wrestlers during his first run in XPW, much like he did in ECW. In 2005, Lazie said that many of the local wrestlers whined about his training sessions because he was an outsider coming in and telling them what to do. However, Lazie added in 2019 that it was worth it because "You improve just by being in the same room with the guy." The agent part had to do with giving advice to younger talent to better themselves. For instance, Messiah mentioned Smothers on Yakuza Kick as being instrumental in teaching him the art of "feeding" for an Irish whip. Smothers, according to Rizzono, alternated whose matches he watched and would ask each wrestler what their finisher was and give them advice on how to do it better. Kloss also told Kaos on an "Xtreme Memories" podcast that Smothers gave him a commentary and ring announcing tip or two.

Hamrick recalls a funny exchange with Smothers while waiting for fans to enter for the Q&A session in January 2003. Smothers was drinking a protein shake and eating a protein bar and Hamrick was consuming a chocolate donut:

SMOTHERS: "You don't ever blow up?"

HAMRICK: "Not really."

SMOTHERS: "Don't you ever work out?"

HAMRICK: "Not really."

SMOTHERS: "I hate you."

Jerry Lynn, like Hamrick and Smothers, was also part of XPW when it folded. The first time he discussed XPW publicly was in a *SLAM! Wrestling* article about the HeatWave incident roughly a month after it happened:

"They were trying to make a name for themselves off of us, but all that came out in the end was that they made fools of themselves, and they embarrassed themselves. There was no way they were going to get any good out of it."

Lynn told me in July 2005 that he felt strongly about his decision to go to XPW, which he says was due to his "personal financial situation." ECW, he explains, had put him in debt because of constantly bounced checks, while the only XPW check that bounced for him was the one for the Pittsburgh show. Furthermore, he says "I'm an independent contractor" and therefore was going to work for whatever promotion was going to feed his family.

Even when he did go to XPW, Lynn clashed with Kleinrock. He says that Kleinrock asked Jonny Storm to do a moonsault off of a balcony with only two of his three opponents catching him, which Lynn thought was too dangerous. He adds that Kleinrock isn't a wrestler and "didn't have a clue" about what being a wrestler was like, so he tried to get wrestlers to do unsafe stunts. Luke has also said that Lynn stuck up for him when Black wanted Luke to absorb unprotected chairshots from Supreme.

Lynn, in turn, got Justin Credible into XPW, although Rizzono mentioned in a February 20, 2001 interview with Peter Hinds that Credible negotiated with XPW after ECW folded and before he ultimately joined WWE. When he did show up in XPW in 2003, Credible, according to his 2003 RF interview, had a deal for $1,500 per night and he agreed not to work for TNA. However, due to bounced checks he only ended up getting paid about $1,000 combined for four XPW shows, missing out on thousands he was owed.

During the 2010s social media years, Credible got back in touch temporarily with Black and permanently with Borden, maintaining contact with her to this day. In his Kayfabe Commentaries *ECW Timeline* edition, he said about XPW management and the idea of bringing it back at the time, "They're out of their minds. They're just people who don't belong in our business." He was referencing Black, although it was not clear whether he was also referring to Borden as well when he said "they're." Credible said this despite being the main draw who had agreed to star in the resurgence of XPW at the exact same time (2013).

Credible's ECW rival Sandman also joined XPW, and in fact even got temporarily banned from wrestling in his home state of Pennsylvania after his behavior at an XPW show in December 2002. Sandman mentioned in his 2004 RF shoot that he had his own locker room at XPW's Grand Olympic Auditorium shows. Luke says that Sandman had a lot to do with hanging the prop weapons from the ceiling for his House of Horrors match vs. Supreme. Pogo The Clown, who worked with him regularly on Philly shows before his ban, said that even though he was always drunk, Sandman never messed up a spot with him. Pogo calls Sandman a "manipulator," but did not elaborate.

Hamrick recalled to me a humorous Sandman anecdote from a week before Hostile Takeover:

"He comes up to me on this indy show and tells me that he has a proposition for me. He tells me that XPW is coming to the Arena next weekend and that he is going to get me on that show. I was like, 'Hak, I am in the semi-main event in a Ladder match for the XPW TV title.' He was like, 'Are you sure?' I told him, 'Yes, that's what they are telling me.' He says, 'Nevermind then.'"

Sandman's ECW rival Sabu also entered XPW. Despite essentially scoffing at the mention of it in his RF interview, Sabu "wanted so badly for XPW to work," according to Lazie, his then-booking agent and ringside manager who became very close with him. Lazie was with Sabu when he buried his dog, went to the home in Japan of his then-wife and ate dinner with them, was involved with his mom when she had health problems, went to the "Crazy Girls" strip club with him after some XPW shows, often lodged him at his house overnight, and was introduced to his uncle The Original Sheik several times. Sabu wrote in his 2019 autobiography that one of the few good things that came out of XPW was that he met Melissa Coates, who he would end up dating about 15 years later.

Byron wrote in a March 2021 facebook post, "All I remember about Sabu is he complained constantly and did a lot of drugs."

Despite Tod Gordon falsely claiming in a December 8, 2004 post on PWInsider.com that ECW never sued Sabu, Heyman and Karel did in fact sue Sabu in a New York court for contract interference, specifically, breach of contract and anticipatory breach, which Sabu confirmed when asked about it on Facebook. This was despite ECW owing Sabu money at the time. Kleinrock recalls that XPW paid thousands of dollars for Sabu's lawyer and legal case, explaining in his SCU interview, "We were ready to go to court. The only reason the ECW case got dropped is because they went bankrupt." So according to Lazie, when Sabu made his debut, XPW tried to pass it off as he wasn't getting paid to avoid worsening the ECW case, although he surely was paid.

ECW never legally pursued Stampede Wrestling, a long-time stalwart in wrestling which was also using Sabu at the same time. It was in Stampede that Sabu and Lazie saw a wrestler do the Sliced Bread #2 move and then described it to Kaos, who started using it. According to Rizzono, backstage at Go Funk Yourself, Sabu demonstrated with the sword that Rizzono and Kaos used in their "I Quit" match how to safely but believably "stab" an opponent. His hands slipped and he cut himself accidentally, and in his match with Terry Funk that night, a bandage on his hand that he frequently adjusts is visible. Rizzono told me he and Sabu discussed doing a tandem that would feature Sabu pointing up and Rizzono pointing down and being called "Tabu."

Besides Canada, Sabu (often managed by Lazie) also defended his XPW title throughout the U.S., England, and Mexico, acquiring XPW publicity. Mexico's Xtreme Latin American Wrestling (XLAW) alone hosted multiple title defenses by Sabu against Damian 666, and there's a story behind those defenses, according to webmaster Tony T. "At just about every XPW card, Damian 666 would try and get Sabu to work Mexico with him. Sabu declined every time." One day, Lazie offered Sabu tacos. Sabu asked "What is a taco?" A shocked Lazie explained. "Sabu then agreed to eat three with the hottest sauce available," Tony says. Lazie brought them to Sabu, who looked at them confused before trying one. Then, he ordered Lazie to bring him three more. "Right after Sabu finished wolfing down his sixth taco," he told Damian that he would work in Mexico. Damian, "in disbelief, responded 'Really?' Sabu then replied 'I will work Mexico because I like the food.'"

Sabu and Lazie's March 16, 2001 trip in Mexico, though, didn't go as planned. Without clearing it with Lazie first, Canadian Wrestling Federation (CWF) promoter Ernie Todd announced that Sabu and Lazie would do a polaroid session for fans and radio interviews to promote a show they were on in Canada. They were, Lazie says, willing to do those things, but only for extra money. Upon realizing that he wasn't going to get what he wanted, Todd, Lazie says, called immigration authorities on them. Sabu was separated from his passport. He and Lazie were jailed in Mexico for less than a day, but overnight, and were supposed to leave the country, but instead went to their scheduled show. After cops or immigration were paid off, Sabu snuck into the venue by wearing the mask of El Hijo Del Santo (who was also on the show), wrestled his match, and left, while Lazie was kicked out of the locker room after sneaking in with a mask and had to wait outside.

The day before Sabu left XPW, there was an invitation-only show at Extreme Associates headquarters for Japanese tourists. Sabu and Lazie signed autographs, took photos, and barbecued with the tourists, and there were three matches. Lazie says it was a favor for Fumi Saito of Japan's *Baseball Magazine*, and also partially a favor for FMW's Shoichi Arai, too. Lazie mentions that the show, which mostly he and Sabu organized, got them heat because they were already not getting along with XPW management by that point. Sabu was supposed to wrestle Messiah, but didn't due to Messiah's fallout with XPW (stemming from a real life feud between he and Black regarding an affair with Lizzy Borden) leading up to the show. The next day, Sabu had his last XPW match. Lazie and Sabu didn't know it was their final show until the day of, when a visibly nervous (according to Lazie) Kleinrock told them they'd no longer be needed.

New Jack was, like Sabu among the ECW wrestlers who added most to their career legacies while in XPW. Angel said in a June 3, 2002 XPWTV.com interview, "When New Jack came in [to XPW], I really think he brought a lot of fans with him." Opinions vary about him, though. For instance, Borden said in a May 2008 in-person conversation that Jack was the only XPW wrestler she didn't like because one never knew how he would act on a given day. Also, Kraq said "New Jack had a real ghetto mentality...a hard personality to try to get used to." He is not sure if Jack talked to him like that because he was also black, but overall says "I wouldn't have dinner with that guy." Kraq recounts that after Jack went through a table that was lit on fire, he thought to himself "This will be my chance to get in with New Jack good." So Kraq took vodka out of his own bag and mixed a drink for Jack. He says, "I thought because of his hard personality he should be able to take something like that." Instead, Jack sipped the drink before throwing it and yelling, "Motherfucker, this drink is too strong!"

Kleinrock and Rizzono were on the other end of the spectrum as far as New Jack, with Kleinrock telling SCU, "New Jack was easily one of my favorite people I've ever dealt with in wrestling." Rizzono, meanwhile, was very close with Jack and kept in touch with him on a regular basis until about 2005. Rizzono told me in 2004 that he loved Jack to death and that, "There are three people on this planet in whose hands I would trust my life - my mother, my father, and New Jack." Joking or not, Rizzono sounded completely serious when he said that. Rizzono recounted to False Count Radio how he picked New Jack's hotel room lock one night and splashed a nude Jack on the bed and pinned him with a referee counting the fall. Since he knew he would never be put over Jack, this was his only chance to beat him. Kleinrock told Rizzono of plans to break him away from The Enterprise and team him with Jack, with Rizzono acting like a white gangsta and trying to talk ebonics to an annoyed Jack.

Konnan shared two New Jack stories from XPW with me:

"New Jack rolled up on me mad that somebody had said something supposedly I said about him...After connecting the dots, we figured out he had me confused with some else but he came ready to fight almost on sight. Another time, I had told New Jack I had a song he was gonna love. It had a West coast gangsta beat with some hard lyrics. Anyways, I come out pumped ready to come out to this new song I had spent a lot of time on and when I came out, the DJ played a song by Bow Wow called 'Whats My Name?' which is before Wow hit puberty. It was a song like for kids. When I got back [to the locker room], Jack was waiting for me and gave me shit for a long time afterwards."

Jack would get free Extreme Associates porn videos as gifts. One time at the office, according to Messiah on Yakuza Kick Radio, he bought a tape of the Mass Transit incident and did play-by-play over it for Messiah.

Another person who worked at the office as the accountant was David Pentycofe, who was nicknamed "G-Man." A drunk Pentycofe, who was Caucasian, approached Jack at an after-show party at the Viper Room and supposedly said something like "Let me buy my n*gga a beer," after Jack had previously told him not to use the "n" word around him. Jack proceeded to swing a beer mug at his face and cut him from chin to forehead. Angel was about 20 feet away from it and heard the glass break over G-Man's face.

Former-ECW valet Missy hyatt, when asked about her memories of hanging out in California for XPW, recalled to me:

"The only place I went was with Scotty Schwartz to Jerry's Famous Deli and one time Gene Simmons from KISS was having his birthday party and I took Big Dick [because] he was a fan...I was just there to get out of the house for a few days; I was married at the time... "I was just happy to get to go to LA for a couple of days, eat at some of my old [favorite] places and shop at some of the stores on Melrose and the Beverly Center...One day, [Chastity and I] took a car and I took her to Melrose and up close to the Hollywood sign to take pictures. I think I made her go by my old house there, too. That was sad for me."

Black said on his April 1, 2020 podcast that the first purpose of bringing these ECW names into XPW was to"try to sell some tickets" to people who've never seen a particular name live, and "the other part of the motivation is to give legitimacy to your homegrown talent...and not just 'Oh, here's an appearance and then they leave' because that's the ultimate indie [tendency]...If I was gonna bring in guys, they were going to be there to do a program."

Black was right about this. There were over 15 wrestlers who arguably made their biggest impact on wrestling as midcarders or main eventers in ECW, and also had at least three matches in XPW, and that doesn't even account for lower-card workers in ECW who made multiple XPW appearances. On the other hand, there were only three wrestlers who are arguably best known in wrestling from their ECW tenures who only had one match in XPW: Little Guido, Ian Rotten, and Raven. All three appeared in XPW after the Philly era began, and one of them, Ian, appeared on three XPW shows and did a program vs. Supreme that included the one blow-off match..

Several midcard and lower status ECW wrestlers joined XPW during the Philly era. Danny Doring admitted to Justin Henry in March 2013 that upon joining XPW at Hostile Takeover, he and Chris Chetti "had our guards up" that "we may be being set up" after the HeatWave incident, but instead "everyone was very accepting...from Rob Black down...and it was a good place to be until the wheels rolled off."

Many of the ECW talents who had previously made South Philly's Holiday Inn and Travel Lodge their depraved partying locations were put up in stopovers like the Aku Aku Inn in Woodland Hills and the Airtel Plaza Hotel in Van Nuys. These lodging sites became the host to new forms of debauchery by extreme alum who were on what were in many ways paid vacations out in California.

VIC GRIMES SPEAKS ON THE NEW JACK FREEFALL INCIDENT

'I was never afraid to dive off that thing. I was never afraid to do any of the crap that he ever said'.

Vic says he used to work for a scaffolding company before he was a wrestler, so he's not scared of heights.

'I didn't plan it to go wrong or anything, it just did. but everyone knows when you wrestle, there's a chance things can go wrong' - about Danbury

'We didn't wrestle too much after that because of the fact that he really wanted to hurt me for real. he hated me. we even got in a fight in a locker room one time.'

'And basically he goes to pick me up and throw me off but literally I don't care what they say...you aint gonna pick up a 350 pound man off the ground and throw a person if he doesn't wanna go...Obviously I didn't get thrown off. I threw myself off. I made it look good...I could see everything as I was coming down and when I actually hit I knew I was hitting the turnbuckle area and when I bounced, I actually knew to tuck my left shoulder and my chin and

turn inward to try to land in the ring. If I wouldn't have done that I woulda bounced and flipped out onto the floor and probably broke my neck'

8. Extreme Associates & Porn Stars

Everyone who worked for XPW knew about its porn connection. Even the foreigners knew, with Kikuzawa saying that the porn link was not a secret - "we understood." The Gurentai member recalls one instance, he thinks at the Metal Fest concert show, that he went to the merchandise table and saw a porn video sitting there, and it was then that he internalized that XPW was owned by a porn company.

Tammy Lynn Sytch said in a June 2007 In Your Head interview that she didn't like that there was so much overlap in the staff between Extreme Associates and XPW and that as a result,

"They really didn't know what they were doing as far as doing a wrestling show." She said that even though XPW had "nice people," there were "whackos," too. Major Gunns, who years later did porn, also mentioned in a February 2006 Wrestling Epicenter interview that she wasn't thrilled upon learning that XPW was so intricately connected to a porn company.

She was right about the overlap. Several XPW personalities also worked at EA, including Messiah, Damien Steele, Angel, GQ Money, TJ Rush (a friend of GQ's from Colorado), Scott Snott, Jake Lawless, Homeless Jimmy (the front desk secretary), and Webb. TJ and Lawless worked in the warehouse, Jimmy was the front desk secretary at the office, and Snott did a porn scene with an elderly woman and directed four EA films.

Lawless, did porn scenes with Kristi Myst and Jessica Darlin, meanwhile, and Lawless recalls that one of the scenes happened in a Las Vegas hotel room when Myst and Darlin were on ecstasy. Byron was said by Lawless to be so drunk that he couldn't read the blackjack cards. They were shooting a dildo scene and Lawless thought "Fuck it. I'll jump in." So did the cameraman, Derek. Lawless recalled in an April 1, 2020 facebook post that EA even provided him with health insurance, and GQ has also praised the fantastic health insurance he had during his time there, while other employees said they didn't have health insurance.

Not surprisingly, EA had its fair share of colorful characters. Among the most famous was Tom Byron. Konnan recalled on his Keepin It 100 podcast that "it was very weird to see Tom Byron standing there watching fuckin' what we were doing when everybody in that dressing room had seen this motherfucker before [in pornos]." Lazie mentions that even though Byron was generally "a man of few words," on the rare occasion that he did speak, he would, as Kleinrock also mentioned in a 2000 *LA New Times* article by Luke Y. Thompson, say something either so insightful or funny that "it would blow your mind." Pogo says Byron was "hard to read" and Rivera says he was hard to get to know, but that they sometimes found common ground talking about bands.

Luke Hawx says that Byron would sit there drinking alcohol while Hawx would sit with him drinking water. Kristian Blood recalled that the porn legend would spread his arms out like Superman as his way of saying "What's up?" to Blood. Kraq says he had fun driving Byron's Merecedes for a TV show skit. Angel called Byron the "mellow...quiet guy in the back" who "chimed in every so often", and "never raised his voice at anybody." He would send Angel as his "runner" to a local deli to get him sandwiches. Steele, Lazie, Angel, Kaos, and GQ all mentioned to me Byron's pot fandom as sticking out about him, and several people told me that Byron was just a regular guy along for the wrestling ride. While he did on-screen scenes with them all, Byron wrote in January 2018 on facebook that he also dated or was otherwise romantically linked off-screen to Myst, Darlin, and Veronica Caine at various times.

Ron Jeremy was another famous porn star linked to XPW. He had his own in-ring segment on some early shows called "The Casting Couch," in which he interviewed wrestlers. He even did a comedy tour with GQ, called "Ron Jeremy's S&M Sideshow," that spanned several years, including after XPW folded. Some photos have circulated through the years of Jeremy wearing XPW t-shirts at non-wrestling events.

Then there were the women, and there were two categories of X-Girls (as XPW called them) who were part of XPW on-screen - established wrestling valets and porn stars who became on-air seconds. Nicole Bass, who was brought in by Big Dick Dudley, is the only woman who entered as a wrestling act, but got involved in the EA business by filming some bondage videos. According to her Wrestling Universe shoot interview, when she was first asked about doing one particular video with Kronus, Bass demanded that the former-Eliminator test negative for diseases, knowing that he was expected to bleed for the video. She says that Kronus tested "clean as a whistle," to her surprise. The video features Bass throwing Kronus into and over couches, punching him, and talking vulgarly to him. There was also footage shot, but never released, of Bass as a dominatrix beating up Homeless Jimmy with a cane and paintball gun (at close range).

WWE actually attempted to compel discovery of that EA footage in its Bass lawsuit. Graphic summaries (for example, "Bass pours barbeque sauce on a man in a diaper and breaks eggs on his head.") of the footage was printed in legal filings, according to David Bixenspan, who wrote in a December 2017 Deadspin article, "from both the files and the case's docket there does not appear to be an official ruling on this discovery dispute." However, that didn't stop ExtremeAssociates.com from teasing that Black would be subpoenaed.

Damien Steele, who Bass bodyguarded for on camera, said that she was ill-equipped for the on-camera role she was assigned, not seeming to have learned anything about the physical aspects of wrestling before coming to XPW. Messiah, who worked with her on early shows, seemed to agree on Xtreme Memories. As far as her behavior outside of the ring, Webb indicated on Rubber Guard Radio in April 2008 that Bass was the only outside talent who wasn't "low drama." Besides calling her "a bit needy," he remarked specifically "[her husband was] kind of a handful, in a pain in the ass sort of way, and she was, too. They weren't mean-spirited or anything. They were just kind of nutty."

There was a report in the December 27, 1999 *Wrestling Observer* that Bass had heat with fellow future-ECW valet Missy Hyatt over them having a similar look of white shirt and denim shorts. Hyatt, though, had positive things to say about Bass when I spoke to her in March 2006, and when asked about XPW, told me "I think Big Dick said they were trying to get TV so they could try to open a territory - same old stuff all people say."

The second type of wrestler valets in XPW were those who first made their names as porn stars. Big Dick explained the philosophy for using porn stars on screen in his Wrestling Universe shoot interview, saying "Instead of making girls, you've got girls that are already made - adult models that everyone wants to see anyway...It's not any different from [ECW] having Francine and Beulah, except you've got established adult models."

One of those porn stars was Jasmin, who was a big part of XPW's early days. Jasmin said in her 2000 RF Video shoot interview that Black "was really like a brother to me at one point and

I felt like we were family," and that she "did grow very fond of his parents...and his dad was nothing but nice to me--treated me like a daughter." Dynamite D recalled an anecdote that demonstrates the issues between Black and Jasmin:

"Jasmin and Rob's working relationship was always rocky. I remember back in 1998 when we were meeting with Rob (and Tommy) at the first EA offices, she was on the phone. Rob was having trouble with her, arguing and trying to convince her everything was alright. When he hung up the phone, he told us she was threatening him with her performance and if she didn't get what she wanted, she was going to be a 'dead fuck,' which basically means she would just lay there and not 'act' into it, etc. This prompted me to suggest if this happens, he casts her as the lead in 'Night of the Living Dead (Fuckers).' We all laughed."

Tension also developed between Borden and Jasmin. Borden once told a story in an online chat circa 2006 about how she got so mad at Jasmin at a porn shoot in Brazil that she almost pushed her off of a roof. At the time, Jasmin's tensions with Black, Borden, and others led to Jasmin leaving Extreme and XPW for ECW, and she also, in an unidentifiable interview, would blame her departure in part on Lazie. Jasmin claimed in interviews that she quit, while Black insisted that he fired her. The debate over what happened dominated some porn dirt sheets for a short while.

Damien Steele also had a rocky relationship at times with Jasmin. Steele began his XPW tenure being managed by cohorts Jasmin, Bass, and "Bad Boy" Basil Bozinis, the latter two of whom have since died. The storyline association between Jasmin and Steele crossed over into real-life, by all accounts. Rizzono said in a phone conversation that Jasmin "had the hots for him." Depending on who you talk to, it may not have been one-sided, as another wrestler (herein referred to as Anonymous Wrestler) says that "[Steele] loved being seen at personal appearances with her. What an ego stroke [it must have been for him]." Jake Lawless (Steele's storyline ally) agrees, saying "Personally, I think at first he liked the attention [from Jasmin], but little did he know that this could be more than any normal male could handle."

Besides Jasmin, another porn star on XPW's debut show was Kristi Myst. Christopher Daniels, who met her through Hamrick during the Southern Comfort member's brief relationship with her after she left XPW, says that he never would've thought Myst was a porn star if he hadn't been told she was. On one of the early XPW shows, there was to be an angle in the ring where a Hierarchy member was to "try" to rape Myst, but Steele and Mike Modest refused to do it. Modest recalled in an October 2008 In Your Head interview that "They wanted me to come out there and hold this chick down and he was gonna rip off her clothes...This was right in the middle of the ring." He said "I got a lot of heat about" refusing to do it, and elaborated on it in an interview with Ken O'Neill. "The day I refused to do the rape angle, Rob really tried to pressure me into it and I wasn't going for it," Modest told O'Neill. "It put a real strain on an otherwise good relationship." Lawless was the one who went through with the attempted rape angle.

Hierarchy member Bass said in her shoot interview that Myst acted like she had "one brain cell" and would do anything she was asked to do. Modest recalls to O'Neill that he "got to watch her play strip poker against five dudes in the locker room before a show. She played a good game, but she LOST." Candido and Tammy have said in interviews that during their first XPW run, they traveled with Myst, Axl, Sabu, and Lazie. Myst was said to be very quiet by travel companion Candido in his Wrestling Universe shoot: "She never spoke. She would just sit there quiet for hours."

Lazie dated Myst on and off during their XPW run. Lazie - who says he once directed an EA film "to prove that any idiot could direct a porno" - mentions about Myst, "It's sad the way she was treated and the way she let herself be treated." He was specifically referring to Black and Borden, adding that Byron was the only person of those three who treated her nicely. Rizzono concurred that she was generally treated horribly. Lazie said they were together day in and day out and that because she didn't like the porn business and would go home and cry, he took steps to distance her from it.

Lazie claims that Black would sometimes send Myst to give a sexual favor to someone he needed to endear himself to. Once Lazie and Myst started dating, Lazie says he told Black, "Dude, this is my girlfriend. The movies are fine, but the extracurricular stuff-- You can't have her doing that shit anymore." He says he and Black had a heated talk in a car one time about this topic where Lazie insisted Myst couldn't give out sexual favors anymore. Black, Lazie says, didn't like the idea that she couldn't be used that way anymore, but agreed only because Lazie was his friend and he wanted to do his friend right. At that point, she stopped providing sexual favors.

Another factor that played into Lazie's eventual departure was an incident that centered around Myst. She had been filmed for the movie "Cocktails" drinking a concoction of bodily fluids, but Lazie destroyed the master tape. He said in 2020 "I never saw what was on the tape," but that "she was really freaked out, and she never got freaked out about anything she filmed. She asked me to do it. So, I did." Black apparently was furious trying to find the tape, until he found out what happened to it. At that point, the material was supposedly re-filmed, but not before Lazie's relationship with Black deteriorated further.

In early November 2000, Myst was announced in porn dirt sheets as being let out of her contract, per her request, by EA, despite having 18 months remaining on it. "We appreciate everything Kristi has done for us," Black told Gene Ross. Apparently, she had second thoughts for a month or so, but in January 2001, she officially departed from EA and XPW, this time for good. Black told Ross at that time, "It was an amicable split and one that will benefit both parties in the long run...We'll all miss Kristi here at Extreme. We wish her the best of luck in her further endeavors."

Porn star Jessica Darlin also entered the wrestling side of affairs, becoming Webb's second XPW valet after Hyatt. Webb says that Darlin really wasn't cut out for wrestling, and that while he is happy that his XPW TV segments with her came out funny, she was always nervous, shy, and really seemed to be suddenly "thrust into a new world." Darlin told me in 2020 that Webb was funny and always made her laugh. She seemed to agree with him about there being some challenges in jumping from porn to wrestling, remarking that it's "not like what it is on TV" when she was watching WCW and GLOW as a child from the safety of her couch. She says that as a valet, wrestling is "very hard" because you have to "remember your part" and balance "tons of different personalities all in one place."

Darlin is right about that, as she interacted with a wide variety of XPW members in her role. She'd do Pogo's makeup at times ("We'd laugh and have so much fun together.") and mentioned Kaos and Lazie as people she interacted with backstage. She said that Gary Key (TOOL) "was a wonderful soft spoken guy that was very caring with me during a match and [would] check me after to make sure I was all still in place." Messiah, meanwhile, recalled in his AWS shoot interview in 2003 that Darlin was fearless and would pick a fight with anyone, regardless of whether it was New Jack or a fellow porn star. Darlin mentions that she did not get paid extra for XPW appearances; she simply participated for fun.

Veronica Caine, meanwhile, was the last EA actress to join XPW in a major role, although she had been to some XPW shows before that. Lazie said that she was at a Hollywood Palace XPW show flashing from the upper balcony, so he went up and kicked her out of the building. Veronica herself said on the March 22, 2003 edition of Xtreme Mayhem Radio that she was with EA when she assisted (presumably doing ring crew duties, although she didn't specify) at a Reseda Country Club show, which would have been 1999. So, she had been to XPW shows before debuting on camera.

Caine, who dated Webb, managed the Enterprise stable on screen. Rizzono said she had more personality than Myst and that she was "very easy to work with and an absolute sweetheart." As she elaborated on in a December 22, 2002 XMR interview, even the fans in California or Philly differed from one another:

"[The Philly crowd has been] kind of therapeutic for me. I've been able to get more interactive with them and sling insults back and forth with them and it's kind of fun, whereas in LA, everyone's so about being cool and being beautiful that it just wasn't as fun here...If somebody told me in the LA crowd that they wanted to kill me [like a fan did in Philly recently], I'd have security tell them to leave because I take them more seriously. They're just a little more bitter."

She had similar comments on her appearance a few months later on the same show:

"I wasn't as much of a sweetheart in Philadelphia...I was like a different person than I was in California because I had my defenses up. The California crowd was rough so I thought the Philly crowd was gonna be a lot worse, and they really weren't. They're a lot funner. They're just as vocal, but they're not as hostile and vacant.."

Veronica left XPW in early 2003 between the January double-header (her last shows) and the Valentine's Day show, around the same time Webb left. She was with XPW beyond the end of her EA tenure. Veronica said in her early 2003 XMR interview that she stopped doing adult scenes about six months earlier, which approximately coincides with the timeline of circa late 2002 when Douglas started doing media interviews saying that the XPW women were no longer doing porn scenes. Douglas admitted on the October 8, 2019 "Franchised with Shane Douglas" podcast that "one of the agreements Rob and I had was that we had to make a clear separation" between EA and XPW because "keeping those two [companies] closely associated would make it too easy to criticize" XPW.

On her March 2003 XMR interview, Veronica even referenced a backstage "pep talk" by Douglas before the fan Q&A regarding "how we should field the questions if we can't handle them and he kept referring to porno questions...Even Lizzy and I both were like 'Oh, really? Oh, I see. [Porno money is] good enough to make the company, but now we're gonna not mention it.'" Veronica also mentioned in that interview, about Lizzy, "I don't even think she's directed anything for a while." So, there were definitely attempts to distance XPW from the porn as the Philly era wore on, which was a far cry from the early days when the porn connection was openly embraced.

There was always slight tension that saw Kaos and GQ together and Veronica on a separate side, as Veronica explained on XMR in March 2003:

"There was that [tension] from the beginning. They immediately bonded and, you notice when we do interviews with them, it's them, and then me. Right off the bat, they formed their little ambiguously gay duo. Everyone in the Extreme offices would call them 'Ace and Gary' because they were constantly on each other's nuts...There was a brief period of time where we were all really together, but there's just a lot of ego going on there."

She became friends outside of the ring with GQ and Kaos, although at one point there was a falling-out specifically between herself and GQ. He explained in October 2003:

"I know she thinks I stabbed her in the back or whatever, and I'm sorry she feels that way, but the fact is, I do value that she took me under her wing when I first got to Cali, looked out for me, and taught me the ropes. She was definitely my first friend there, and even though we drifted, I value the friendship she gave me."

One reason for the issues between the two may have had to do with how Veronica's departure from XPW was explained on XPW TV. In her March 2003 XMR interview, she said about her departure:

"I don't know if it was [portrayed negatively] necessarily by the company or by GQ Money and Kaos. Pretty much GQ Money, I think. I found out it was portrayed in a really derogatory light, like that I supposedly died doing coke off of their penises...I thought 'Well, probably the reason they're going with that is because I left and it's more of like an XPW angle to be like "Yeah, fuck her. She walked away, so we'll say she died on crack or whatever,"' but then I found out they came on your show recently and they're still going with that whole lie, so I don't know. I know they feel the need to live their gimmicks 24/7...I just thought that was a little out of line considering what was really going on."

Veronica and GQ seem to have made up during the Facebook social media years.

GQ was able to speak first hand about how the EA office had its wild moments, for sure, but was also very demanding, reminiscing to me in March 2003:

"It was fun, it was fast paced, it was wild, it was hard work, and it was exciting. You never knew what was going to happen, and anything could happen. It was like a sitcom, or a movie, or a drama show all rolled into one...Hard work was an important quality, and getting shit done took priority over fun. So, it's not like it was this huge party."

What was a party, though, was the night of the X-Rated Critics Organization (XRCO) awards show in April 2002, when EA won what would generally be considered the least desirable award. GQ recalled "They sent me up to accept the award for 'Worst Movie of the Year.' All hell broke loose when I went off on a freestyle rap acceptance making fun of everyone, and staking Extreme's claim as the best, and the most extreme, complete with me bumping on the stage." Kaos was there with the TV title, and so was Veronica and Byron, as well as GQ's seven-foot friend from Colorado, who was working for EA and appeared one time for XPW as "Exodus."

Messiah has spoken of the high pressure environment of EA by saying in interviews that even though there was never a day there that he didn't "laugh [his] ass off," there was also never a day that he didn't want to punch someone in the face out of frustration. In fact, in his SMV "Best on the Indies" shoot interview, he said that EA was "a very hostile work environment" and compared it to a "mafia" atmosphere in that once you were gone from "the family," regardless of whether you left "on good terms or bad terms," there was no coming back.

Angel had similar words to me about mafia resemblance, saying how people would call the office with threats that if Black didn't pay them in two hours, they would show up with baseball bats. Angel even got assigned to driving a suspicious bag (which he could tell was always full of cash, although he never opened it) out to Thousand Oaks an hour and a half away as a weekly Friday job. "The less I knew, the better because if they ever got me in court," he would deny knowledge and he wouldn't be lying because he really didn't know the details of the situation.

Even though he was only there for a few months, Phenomenal Phil summed up the atmosphere at the Extreme Associates office very succinctly on his Xtreme Memories episode:

"You go up and down that card of wrestlers and it's like, 'He slept with her. She slept with him. They ended up getting divorced. There was this affair. There was that affair...He wanted to sleep with her. This guy did porn'...It was a very loose culture at XPW. There was drug use, there was white powder on tables and it smelled like weed all the time, and there was a bottle of piña colada mix…[Another time], there was a porn [video] that was filmed in our wrestling ring in the warehouse and it wasn't just normal porn; it was enema porn, in our ring that we had to wrestle in, and so we [wrestlers] had like a mini-mutiny. We were like 'We're not doing this. We're not wrestling in this ring where there was an enema going on and there was porn being filmed, and Rob's like 'Ah, come on, it's not a big deal.'...That office was like stepping into another dimension."

In the case of the enema porno in the ring, they ended up buying a new ring canvas.

As atypical as life at the office was compared to other businesses, Lawless recalled on Xtreme Memories that those who worked there didn't gossip much because they got used to the unusual work environment:

"I worked at other places afterwards. In that [porn] business, if someone hooks up for a night, the next day it was like 'Oh, that was fun' and that was about the end of it. Every other business I've been to, all they do is gossip about who's dating who, and I'm going 'Damn, it was refreshing because no one really even cared about it.'"

EA business would be conducted between 9 am and 5 or 6 pm and XPW business after 5 or 6 until as late as the middle of the night. Jimmy said on Xtreme Memories "I was there from morning...until night time, until the next morning" and Kloss followed up by saying that sometimes by the time he left the office, the sun would be comin up. Kleinrock has said in interviews that during the XPW era, he used to frequently work 18-22 hour days. Tracy Smothers backed that up in his SMV shoot interview that took place weeks after what ended up being XPW's final show, saying "Kevin works hard. He's working 80-90 hours a week," and Mike Hartsfield said in his 2021 Xtreme Memories interview that Kleinrock was "*always* working, and not just sitting at the office saying 'Hey, I'm at work.' [He was] working and working till all hours." Konnan called him "a workaholic" to me and Kleinrock even wrote himself in a column on XPWrestling.com on January 27, 2001 "I spent all of 2000 without a single vacation day." To excel at Extreme Associates, you needed to be willing to work hard, although many staff played hard, also.

7. *Boss culture*

Rob Black got along with most of his talent. There was by the account of both sides plenty of mutual respect between Black and wrestlers who worked in the office, especially Webb and GQ Money, both of whose podcast comments have defended Black. While Webb said in a December 2008 In Your Head interview about Black that "When you first meet the guy and whatnot, everybody pretty much, he'll make you feel like you're his best friend in the world, but when things go bad, then things get ugly," he has also been positive about him at times. Webb indicated in an April 2008 Rubber Guard Radio interview that Black did not have "trust issues" with the talent that had chosen to be loyal to him by having "never really questioned the whole concept of being exclusive" to XPW. Black, Webb says, was willing to "reward" some of those talents by letting them work with big former-ECW names who came into the company.

GQ echoed those sentiments a few weeks later on a May 18 edition of False Count Radio and defended Black by saying that he "looked out for guys that he cared about and who cared about him." Kleinrock had similar comments in an Xtreme Memories interview in July 2020, saying "If you were one of the people who were loyal to Rob, he took care of you," and so did Douglas to RF Video in 2003 - "One thing I'll say about Rob is he was loyal to his guys because he wouldn't cut them [when the budget called for it]." Altar Boy Luke had a polar opposite opinion on Xtreme Memories, saying about Black, "There wasn't [any] loyalty, even to the people that were being loyal," and Kloss followed up the comment by remarking that loyalty in XPW could be a double-edged sword sometimes.

Insight into Kloss's relationship with Black has shown itself in various podcasts. On the Phenomenal Phil Xtreme Memories edition, Kloss said that Black succeeded in maintaining "a good balance" of the "ego-driven" nature of pro wrestlers that a promoter needs to "control" and his own need to "turn it up and then [say] 'Nah, remember who's the boss here'" (all Kloss' words). On August 25, 2014 "Kris Kloss Show," he recalled that "we had a boss that...we didn't like all the time, but we respected, we feared, but we wanted to please him because we also knew what he was doing for us." Kloss explained that "you don't want to make him mad...and he's got this Al Capone 'I'm gonna fucking kill you' attitude when he's talking to you." However, Kloss told Kraq on Xtreme Memories that Black's "ballbuster" and "drill sergeant" attitude "toughened a lot of us up and we gained a thick skin because of it." In fact, he added on the Hernandez edition of Xtreme Memories that mutual creative engagement was especially possible when you got past "the rough around the edges part of Rob" that intimidated some people: "When you got to the point with Rob where you can crack a joke and lighten the mood, those were the times where you can really share ideas."

Kraq, who featured Kloss as the best man at his wedding, was another person who wanted to impress Black as thanks for the special opportunity that the Extreme Associates head honcho had given him on-screen in XPW. Kraq told me that he knows that Black didn't have to do what he did for him by giving a shot in

XPW, as he realizes he didn't pay any dues and "was in the right place at the right time." He adds that Black "was always approachable when I needed anything from him" and "I could talk to him about anything." Someone told Kraq that he was the first black person who got to go into Black's house. Angel, Kraq's storyline boyfriend, says that with any other boss who made who made "racist jokes" and the like, "you'd be going to HR" saying "this guy shouldn't be talking like this," but that it came with the territory with Black. Angel remembers that in Philly at times, Black would take the whole roster out to a meal and pay for it on his own dime.

Black elaborated on the "perks" (his words) that "some of the workers got" on an April 1, 2020 podcast. He emphasized that "I couldn't show favorites" and say that someone's "better than" someone else and "gets special treatment over" their colleague. There were "a set of rules for everybody," but that didn't mean that he wouldn't take certain people out to dinner, or let certain roster members "come to my house or watch football" as rewards for their efforts in the office. Kikuzawa recalls going to Black's house and seeing a big swimming pool and thinking, "Oh, so this is how people live in the U.S." Black also paid for Webb to go to video editing school and learn production skills, and then gave him a job in the office. So, Black was willing to invest in the morale of his local talent. Messiah even said on Xtreme Memories that Black paid Supreme while he was out of action due to his fire injury.

In addition to maintaining positive terms with his California roster members, Black needed to appease the outsiders who came into the company so that they would keep coming back, and consequently, some ECW veterans have praised Black in interviews. Sandman told RF Video in 2004 that "I like Rob Black. He did whatever I asked him to." Similarly, Terry Funk told RF Video in 2003 that Black "treated me [as] nice as anyone's ever treated me in my life." and Candido his 2001 SMV shoot looked back on his first XPW tenure (2000) as Black having "always treated us fantastically." Axl Rotten also had largely kind words about Black to In Your Head Radio in 2006, saying "Black was nothing but cool to me" and "he's always been straight up business with me." Granted, though, Axl also told John Mikels in 2005 that he "[had] no opinion one way or the other" on Black.

While Jessica Darlin said in 2020 and 2021 that Black "was a great boss" to her ("He was always nice to me. Funny. We were always close like family. [We] still talk to this day."), former-ECW valets Missy Hyatt and Tammy Lynn Sytch, on the other hand, had negative things to say about Black. In her 2001 Wrestling Universe shoot, Hyatt called Black a "moron," a "jabroni," an "idiot" (twice), an "asshole," and a "scumbag." Kristian Blood told me that Hyatt tried to give Black advice on how to run XPW, but Black supposedly didn't appreciate it. Sytch, meanwhile, said in a 2006 Wrestling Epicenter interview that Black even mentioned on her very first XPW show that he would pay her to do porn, and she also criticized her XPW paydays.

Nicole Bass was another former-ECW woman who developed problems with Black, specifically as it relates to the bondage movies she did for EA. In a May 4, 2000 AVN article called Bass Blown Out Of Extreme Waters, Bass described how Black's treatment of her evolved from limo-style to third-rate:

"First time I went out there, I was treated very well. The second time I was out there, I was treated very well. The third time we go out there, this [Josh] Lazie guy starts appearing. The fourth time is kind of strange. The fifth time? Before, I would be doing all the scenes in one day. This time it took three days with 12 hour days. I was exhausted after three days. I asked for a day off. Lazie said 'That's it; we're even. I don't owe you nothin'. You don't owe us nothin'...The only time Rob calls you back is when he wants something...I've heard all the excuses Rob gave. Rob says to me, 'I blew all my money on you.' I was the one who said 'I charge $3,000 to do a tape' and Rob said, 'I'll pay you six.' Now I'm getting yelled out because he feels he got ripped off? Because I didn't jump and go on *The Howard Stern Show* [and promote him]?"

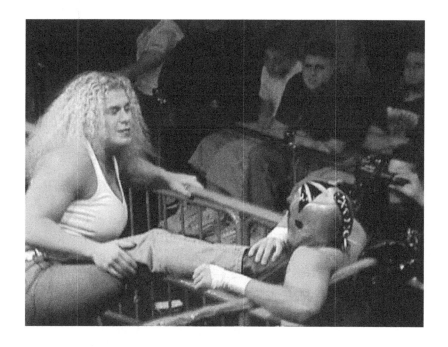

Black gave his side to AVN:

"The deal was she was supposed to be on Howard. That's the bottom line...Every time she's been out here, I've paid for her fuckin' hotel room; I've paid for her fuckin' husband Bob to fuckin' eat. I probably got like $50,000 into the fuckin' project...You can never say I didn't pay her. She got paid astronomically. Nobody gets that for...bondage money, but I did that figuring she'd be on Stern...I gave her six grand to do a movie; then she would wrestle and she'd make another fuckin' two or three thousand on top of that...She can't say she got fucked out of money. The videos weren't doing what they were supposed to do...Nicole Bass cost me more than Tammy and Chris Candido put together, and she wasn't drawing. When we first started we needed to get all the star power. But now we're established. Everybody's got to pull their weight. She didn't pull her weight. It wasn't cost effective. I'm a businessman, not a fuckin' mark."

Lazie agrees about Bass not being worth what she was being paid, saying in 2019 "I think she wasn't the draw [Rob] expected and that money could be better used elsewhere." In regards to her complaints to AVN about Lazie specifically, he says the buck stopped with Black: "I had no problem with her. I just think Rob wanted her gone. Unfortunately, it was my job to get rid of people."

Lazie told me that Black certainly didn't treat the homegrown talent terribly, but he also definitely didn't spoil them like he did the big names. Sabu, who Lazie managed on-screen, and Black had a multitude of problems, so much so that Sabu did most of his business through Lazie while in XPW. This included talking money, as Sabu was asked by Lazie when he entered the company what his fee was and gave a high number. Lazie brought it to Black and says that because Black was "a mark" and just wanted Sabu on his shows, he agreed to it. So, for much of his XPW run, according to Lazie, Sabu got a larger amount of money than he did at many other shows, but Black eventually figured it out and Sabu took a pay cut. Sabu mentioned on Xtreme Memories about Black that "towards the end [of my XPW tenure], I couldn't stand...being around him."

In mid-2001, Black needed to find a way to get the XPW title off of Sabu, which was easier said than done because according to Lazie, Sabu wasn't willing to lose the title to the number one candidate, Messiah. So, one time when Sabu was overseas without Lazie, New Jack defended the title for him and Messiah won the belt by defeating Jack, the "substitute" champion. When Sabu was told about the title change, Lazie said he was pissed off because it was done without consulting him, but he was also somewhat relieved, supposedly telling Lazie something like "Well, I sure as hell wasn't going to lose it to Billy (Messiah)." So, while Eric Gargiulo boasted on CZW commentary that Messiah had never lost the XPW title, technically he also never beat the reigning champion to properly acquire it in the first place. Black indicated to me in 2013 that he strongly dislikes Sabu and said in a September 2019 TeenSetRadio interview with Will Carroll that "Sabu was such a miserable human being." Sabu, Lazie says, is still owed a few thousand dollars by Black. Will would later be appointed to a prominent position by Black in 2021 taking part in XPW's eventual relaunch, with Black and Sabu reconciling as Sabu would be honored at their Beautiful Disaster event.

While many XPW personalities, like Kraq and Kloss, have a more positive opinion of Black than Hyatt, Sytch, and Sabu and have pointed to Black being instrumental in building their careers, the negative stories often seem to get more play in interviews. There are certain examples of specific talents going on the record as saying they had notable disputes with him. On his May 6, 2020 podcast, Black emphasized that he had positive intentions, saying "I could be nasty. I mean I wasn't necessarily 'Horrible Bosses' Kevin Spacey nasty, but I definitely could be a person's dream killer...but it was only because I wanted the best."

Black has commented various times on the idea that he had "heat" in the XPW locker room saying on facebook on March 31, 2020 to Jake Lawless, "Others were with me for double, triple the time [as you were]. I gave them [their] starts, taught them skills, and the first chance they got to fuck me or bad mouth me, they did [because] at the time, it was the cool thing to do." He also admitted in the facebook post part of what GQ and Kleinrock said - that he was loyal to his allies, but added that when people were vindictive toward him, he was vindictive in return: "The one thing about me was I gave my people the world, but the first time they fucked me or were disloyal, I was done with them, and if they hurt me, I made sure I hurt them back ten times." He said the same thing on a May 14, 2021 podcast, and on April 1, 2020 that went so far as to say "I never had heat with 90% of the people that other people said I had heat with...That just wasn't the case."

Certain wrestlers have claimed themselves to have had complex relationships with Black. One of them was McMillan. Part of the reason for that, according to McMillan, was due to the "Mr. '80s" aspect of the Dynamite D persona. "Workers would come up to me in the locker room, I mean, guys like Sabu, would shake my hand and then quickly ask me who was I going to be today," McMillan said. "He loved and so did all the boys. This did not sit well with Rob." At Go Funk Yourself, McMillan pitched the idea of impersonating Junkyard Dog or Paul E. Dangerously, but Black rejected both ideas. McMillan said it was one of

"[Black's] many mistakes in my book and yet another one of my genius on-the-spot suggestions."

He also told me that "Rob hated me for saying 'No' to [portraying gay gimmick] Percy Fabulous." McMillan said he thought that the So-Cal Jobbers Union angle was a manner for Rob "to give me shit, and I think he wanted me to leave, or not be around when he was around." He also said that in general "XPW had a way of dragging you down and draining you of the love you had for wrestling. I guess you could say most guys were 'Robbed' of their love for the business." He added, "pun intended."

Black gave his taken on McMillan on his May 6, 2020 podcast:

"I wish we could have done things differently with [him] sooner than later because the character that D created later and D getting his body into shape later would have been a lot more beneficial and would have worked a lot sooner if it would have been from the very beginning."

D's cousin Jimmy has also gone on record as saying that he and Black didn't always see eye to eye during the XPW days. Jimmy stated on The Death Hour podcast in January 2020, "He had a lot of animosity toward me, I think because I looked a lot like him." In an August 2009 In Your Head interview, Jimmy went into more detail:

"Rob didn't think I had it to be the wrestler that I am...We didn't get along very well. From the get-go, he just didn't think I was a wrestler. I guess in his mind I was too short, maybe not in the best of shape, but I proved him wrong...I think he just disliked me even more because I was making it."

Jimmy specifically blamed Black in part for his departure from XPW, saying on In Your Head Radio, "I didn't feel the need to stick around. There were some personal issues...It wasn't for me to be around where somebody disliked me that much. I decided to pack my bags." That being said, Black and Jimmy seemed to get along when Black had Jimmy on as a special guest for his podcast in the mid 2010s.

Early XPW star Kristian Blood told me that he clashed behind-the-scenes with Black in the early days of the organization. Blood said that Black vowed he'd stay behind the camera unlike Heyman. Blood pointed out that this turned out to be false, as he got involved in TV storylines, although in Black's defense, Kleinrock has emphasized on facebook and in some interviews that Black didn't want to be on-screen initially and had to be convinced to become an on-air character. Blood said that Black wanted to "prostitute" the wrestlers, had no respect for them, and would try to sucker them into doing something more extreme every night. Blood claimed to be one of the few to stand up and refuse.

For instance, Blood says that he had an agreement with Black to jump off something 10 feet high on the debut XPW show. Black asked how much higher would he go and Blood said "10 feet, 1 inch" which was his way of saying "Fuck you" to Black. The XPW owner had wanted him to jump from 25 feet and Blood said "Absolutely not." Instead, he jumped off a "mixboard" which was about 12 feet off the floor. During that balcony dive stunt, Hernandez forgot to bring tape to attach Supreme to the table and make it look more believable. When he went up to the balcony to jump off of, Blood heard Black say "He's not going to make it [reach Supreme]." He did make it, but since the table was out too far, he didn't jump high enough and ended up rolling a few times afterwards and got some welts "the size of grapefruits" on his knees. Black had told him to do the "X" motion with his arms before jumping off the balcony, but he forgot to. He also forgot to cut a promo after the match about how XPW was the new face of hardcore wrestling. He had been told to do that a month and a half in advance, but had not been reminded again. So when he got backstage, Black yelled at him for forgetting aspects of the match and Blood snipped back about how nobody reminded him and so it wasn't his fault. He said that being screamed at by Black made him feel disrespected.

Blood recounted messing with Black at times. For instance, at the August 28, 1999 show, Blood (who said he got $150 per show in XPW) said he wore an ECW "Hardcore Café" t-shirt around Black and that angered the XPW boss. Some of the wrestlers even were upset and asked Blood why he did it. Blood was also late to several XPW office meetings because he was a personal trainer and had clients to attend to, and he didn't care that Black didn't like that. One time, Blood came to a meeting and knelt down and kissed Supreme on the head just to get in the head of Black, who Blood said scoffed at the kiss. Another time, Blood called the office and Black picked up and he said "What's up, jadrool?" which is Italian for "low-life" and was Black's favorite word, so he was aiming to give Black a taste of his own medicine. It was on speaker, so Blood heard McMillan, Kaos, Supreme, and others crack up. Blood said that he would hear from people like Donovan Morgan that Black would speak negatively of him behind his back and intentionally make him do jobs.

Damien Steele, a friend of Blood, also stated in 2019 that he had an up-and-down relationship with Black. The pay sheet from the first XPW show that Kleinrock posted on social media in the mid-2010s had dollar numbers for each wrestler except for Big Dick and Steele. Those two names had "(Rob)" written next to them, as if Black was supposed to take care of their pay, and Steele confirmed in 2019 that was indeed the case. However, Steele said in the same interview that once Black realized that Steele "didn't want to partake in the porn shock value rapey side of [XPW], he became angry and thought I was going against the grain."

Until his death, Blood had a check for $988.52 which Black had given to Steele. When he was unable to cash it, Steele asked Blood to cash the check for him. Black suddenly closed the account or stopped paying it or something along those lines, and it left Blood with his credit history marred because it was never paid off. Blood, who was the only XPW alum with whom Steele kept in touch with during the mid 2000s after he left the U.S. for Puerto Rico, said that "Rob promised Tim the world," but that he gave him nothing.

In fairness, though, Black gave Steel multiple jobs. During his first run in the company, Steele worked in the office as his real job, ordering tables, booking venues, and renting video equipment. Then from, 6-8, Steele trained students at Asylum training school in the EA headquarters. He followed Modest and Morgan's APW plan where trainees had to sign a two year agreement. He, of course, also got paid to wrestle for XPW.

Luke's contentious relationship with Black, meanwhile, is evident from many of the former-Altar Boy's interviews. He said on Xtreme Memories that "I was frustrated with Rob; I wasn't frustrated with anyone else." He frequently tells a story of him sitting with Black in the backseat of a car that also included Douglas, after being picked up from the airport. Luke simply greeted Black, who supposedly said "Can you believe I'm actually talking to you?" Luke thought he was just joking, but Black continued "I don't talk to little guys. You've got to prove yourself in this business before I talk to you." Luke wanted to chastise Black back, but knew he shouldn't.

Luke however, did talk back to Black on some other occasions and he thinks that this may have earned him some respect from Black because he wasn't intimidated by him like some were. He said to me that he was one of the few wrestlers not to get "manipulated" by Black. On the May 13, 2008 Rubber Guard Radio episode, Luke summarized his relationship with Black by saying "Rob didn't like me too much because I was a loudmouth, and Rob was a douchebag, and I didn't care for Rob, so I made sure to let Rob know, so he didn't really care for me too much." All of these factors contributed to Luke negotiating with CZW during the Philly run.

Even Luke, though, has given kudos where he thinks they are due. Luke admitted on Xtreme Memories that even he did have to give "credit to Rob Black. I did learn something from him." He was referring to after his match at Fallout, when he won the KOTDM Title. Luke was bloody and injured and immediately headed backstage, where Black yelled at him to "Get back out there!" and milk the the fact that he just "won a fucking belt" and pose for pictures, etc. Luke said that overall he's "thankful that Black gave me an opportunity."

The reality is that Luke is largely right; D, Jimmy, Blood, and Steele all had their greatest successes in wrestling in XPW, and so did all of the homegrown XPW wrestlers, other than arguably Kaos, Messiah, and Luke. Kaos said in a Doorstop Nation interview that a lot of people made promises to him and Supreme during their early days before XPW and "Rob Black was the first guy to say that and actually turn around and do everything he said and it pretty much came true," so there was a gratefulness on some of the XPW wrestlers' parts. Not only did he employ some wrestlers in the office, Black gave also these wrestlers a platform to perform in front of fans, and it was up to them to make the best of it. Some did. Many did not. Two of the most successful characters, Kaos and Supreme, in XPW were also in it the longest of anyone, and that's no coincidence. The cream would eventually rise to the top in XPW, as Black truly promoted a survival of the fittest environment.

10. Philly & Folding

The people who lived it and the fans who followed it remember what it was like. Every day, there was a new story breaking, and more often than not, that story portrayed XPW negatively. The Philadelphia era of XPW was a wild time to be alive. XPWTV.com and CZWfans.com were pitted against each other, but each forum had fans of both companies, something Angel even mentioned in a June 3, 2002 XPWTV.com interview, shortly before XPW went to Philly: "Look at the [XPWTV.com] board. Half of [the fans] are about XPW and half are about CZW. The same thing goes for their [CZWFans.com] boards."

Shane Douglas' return in July 2002 spearheaded XPW's eastbound move to Philly's ECW Arena. Douglas told me in mid-2005 that XPW had initially offered him a six figures annual deal before a four figures per week figure was agreed upon. Douglas said in his August 2002 Wrestling-News.com interview hyping the first Philly show, Hostile Takeover:

"[Black's] exact words to me in hiring me were 'I've spent three and a half years of my life and lots of my money running this company. I've done everything I know to do with it. I don't know how to get it to the next level. I need you to do that.' So, it's just like an alcoholic admitting that he has a problem drinking for Rob Black to admit that he's not the person to take that company to the next level."

On the October 8, 2019 "Franchised" podcast, Douglas said that in XPW, "everybody worked hard, nobody half assed it out there, and there was a camaraderie in the dressing room...[that] felt very similar to ECW." The reason to go to Philly, Douglas told RF Video in 2003, was that XPW management "felt and I felt they had run LA into a ditch hole. They had given LA so much, and so much of it was bad what they had gave LA that I wanted to give LA a break."

Some Californians didn't make the cut to be brought East, particularly Dynamite D and Rizzono. XPW co-founder D ended up in Philly on vacation anyway the weekend of Exit Sandman. D, who was also at the March 1, 2003 LA show, told me:

"I flew myself out, rented a car, drove a lot of the boys around, rented my own room at the hotel. I was trying to set up a meeting with Shane so I could pitch him my ideas for angles, but was not given the time to meet with him."

Douglas explains that D probably went through a third party because if he spoke to him directly, Douglas would never have blown off one of the boys. While Douglas wouldn't have talked to D before the show when things were busy, he would have said to meet him at the hotel after the show and would have talked to him then.

Rizzono, meanwhile, says he was offered a spot on Hostile Takeover, but only if he flew himself out, which he wasn't willing to do.

Going into Hostile Takeover, there were varying accounts as to whether XPW had a promoter's license to run shows in Pennsylvania. Some reports said that they didn't have a license and some said they didn't even know they needed one. Some reports said they were using RF Video's address for their license application, some said they never had RF's permission, and others (including GQ) said RF reneged permission. Some reports said they were using Heritage Wrestling Alliance's (HWA) license and some said HWA reneged. According to Bryant, XPW ended up just getting its own license, but it required jumping through hoops, according to Kleinrock's SCU interview: "I had to fly myself to Philadelphia, drive an hour and a half to the state capital, sit down with the athletic commissioner, and assure him we weren't the devil worshiping, child molesting, evil doers that everyone was saying we were."

GQ told me in September 2003 of the license issue:

"The rules didn't really say you couldn't advertise without having a license. It just said you needed a license before the show. So, we started our advertising campaign. Kleinrock and I went to Philly, met with the advertising guy for TV ads, and met with WGTW about getting a show on TV. We just started promoting, knowing full well we would have our license in time. Then [Bob] Magee started with his shit, but in fact, our translation of the rules meant we hadn't violated anything. People were just jealous that we came into town, had TV, had ads on the WWE shows, and all that."

Douglas gave his take on the license controversy to Wrestling-News.com:

"XPW got a little bit ahead of themself. They weren't quite familiar with the Philadelphia, Pennsylvania rules and they announced the show before they had their license. The rule read that you had to have your license 10 days before the event so they…now know, and they learned the lesson…They spared absolutely no duller expense to go back and hire a lawyer, to fly representatives from the company out on a last minute…They drove personally to Harrisburg to meet with the commission, they met with the bonding company, they put the money up necessary for the bonding. They have handled this thing as professionally as I've ever seen any company handle a situation like that that was admittedly a screw-up, but also admittedly for anyone that's pointing at that and trying to indict XPW has to also then give credit because they handled it so diligently so quickly."

After Hostile Takeover's date was publicized, then-CZW promoter John Zandig announced Tournament Of Death 1 for the same day in Delaware. Even with the competition a state away, Hostile Takeover was largely a success, with a crowd in the high hundreds or low thousands. In a CageMatch.de interview the same year, Hamrick said "It was a packed crowd that was into all the matches. Around the third match, the fans were chanting 'XP Dub!'" Danny Doring even told RF Video that Hostile Takeover "was as close to old ECW" as any other promotion got.

Doring and Joey Matthews both said in their RF shoot interviews that Douglas really talked up XPW to them. Douglas even did not pass up the opportunity to promote some of XPW's stars and overall product during that era when doing media interviews, such as his early 2003 Pro Wrestling Newz 'N Viewz (PWNNV) interview:

"Kaos, who is a young Chris Candido/Franchise-type of character, really has all the tools he needs; all he needs is the exposure. [He is] an exciting performer to watch. Supreme, who's one of the most violent, hardcore guys. He's like an Abdullah The Butcher mixed in with a Taz...Vic Grimes is about a 350 pound man that does moves of a 150 pound guy, and he's incredibly quick and incredibly stealthy in the ring and can move around very well for a man that size and what I found was instead of having a match that I thought was gonna be easy for me to control this guy and have good matches with him, I found that I was having to try to keep up with him because he really is a tremendous performer...What's great about our company is you're gonna see great lucha matches, you're gonna see great wrestling matches, great high-flying matches...At XPW, it's Thanksgiving dinner. You get a smorgasbord of everything."

At Hostile Takeover, there was controversy involving Terry Funk. Douglas told me:

"[Backstage, Funk] said 'Well, how about I...give [Lizzy] a piledriver and then reach up her skirt and pull her panties off and put them over your head?'...My exact words to him were, 'Because this is XPW and because it's owned by a pornography company, if we do that, everyone will say, "See! See! Nothing but pornography!"' and I said 'So, we can't do it.' And he asked me a second time and I said, 'Terry, I would love to let you do it, but I can't. Please understand.' And he says 'Nah nah nah, I'm just kidding with you. I understand. I wouldn't do that.'

"Later that night, he did do that...When he pulls [Lizzy's panties off], Lizzy and I explode in anger. I jump back in the ring and spin him around and tell him to get the fuck out of the ring. And I was very angry, and with every bit of respect I have for him, that was just an absolute direct disrespect to the boss and to the company."

Douglas explained on the October 2019 *Franchised* podcast that an altercation resulted backstage. Grimes threw him a towel to bandage Funk's serious arm injury, but as Douglas turned around to give it to Funk, he received two hard slaps to the ear. Funk ignored his warning not to throw a third shot, which Douglas blocked. As Douglas went to punch Funk himself using his cast-dressed arm, onlookers stepped in. As Douglas said in 2019, Atlas Security "built a wall...shoulder to shoulder, protecting [Funk]," he found "an opening...pushed through...and smacked Terry in the face," knocking him over. Funk ignored Douglas' order to stand back up, so Douglas "slammed his head into the wall." Then, the doctor's threat to have Douglas "arrested" if he touched "my patient again" ended the incident. On "Franchised," Douglas said multiple times that despite lacking proof, he believes Funk was in cahoots with 3PW to cost XPW its license due to the panties removal and especially the heavy bloodletting, and added that "Black always believed that it was an angle that Terry and I were working him on." GQ even said in December 2003, "Shane was yelling. Terry was relaxed...We all wondered if it was a work or not. Still do."

Like Funk, Joey Styles also made one live appearance in Philly. In a December 5, 2002 NoHoldsBarredWrestling.com interview, Styles said he'd be exclusive to XPW and wouldn't work for other promotions. He then left just over a month after joining, on December 22. Douglas, who Kloss says was livid when Styles suddenly resigned, told me in 2005:

"With Joey, you always get 10 different stories. The one thing Joey did that I thought was very unprofessional was the day of one of the Philadelphia shows...we had spent about 15 or 16 hundred dollars on special equipment to bring in so he could do the voiceovers. He called us...one or two o'clock in the afternoon to tell us he wasn't coming, and I thought that was very unprofessional on his part, but he claimed at that time that he had received a check from the company that came from the pornography division...I just think that Joey...took himself a bit too seriously."

A month later, Douglas was asked about Styles at the XPW Q&A session. A fan recap stated that Douglas, like he would also do in a NoHoldsBarredWrestling.com interview a month later on February 23, cited that Styles had scheduling conflicts. That Q&A summary also mentioned that Styles "didn't know how women from his other business would feel about wrestling," but didn't elaborate as to what "women" or "other business" Douglas was referring to.

In a November 2010 YouTube interview with Myke Quest, Styles said "[XPW was] dishonest with me as to where the money was coming from, so when they paid me, I returned the money and **told them not to use that footage going forward**." The last part where he indicated XPW didn't have permission to sell his appearances completely contradicts Styles' Christmas week 2002 announcement on his then-web site 1Wrestling.com that he was departing XPW, which granted consent:

"I had not deposited any of their checks. Therefore, XPW received my announcing services for one live event and three weeks of television gratis. In addition, **XPW has a video featuring my likeness and performance which they can and will sell.**"

Styles didn't return an e-mail and text message request for comment on the discrepancy in 2020.

Kloss told me that a "gracious" Styles told him he felt bad about taking Kloss' spot and that doing so wasn't his intention. Kloss also mentioned that Douglas wanted Styles alone on commentary, but Kleinrock endorsed Kloss. Douglas told me "I don't remember any back and forth with Kleinrock" or "having to fight for or against" Kloss. In late January 2003, Styles claimed that Douglas asked him to report false XPW attendance numbers on 1Wrestling.com.

Leading up to or during the Philly invasion, XPW was accused of trying and failing to raid over 20 combined talents from ROH, CZW, and 3PW, and then there were those that they did end up using. XPW never commented on some of these reports, claimed there was more than meets the eye on others, and denied some entirely.

For instance, Douglas insisted in his PWNNV interview that an allegation that they tried to steal Dusty Rhodes from 3PW "I can categorically state now is false. We never paid Dusty Rhodes any money to not show," likely referring to Rhodes' December 28 3PW no-show. A December 23 Bob Magee report stated that in a December 18 BetweenTheRopes.com interview, Rhodes called XPW money marks, and also reported that "Rhodes refused to return the" message XPW supposedly left with "his secretary."

Also, on a January 2015 "Creative Control" podcast, former-ROH promoter Rob Feinstein talked about what he called the "double payday" opportunity Steve Corino had the night of an ROH show. Feinstein recalled staying "with Steve in the hallway and nobody was around and just going at it with him for like 10 minutes. It wasn't a heated argument fight; it was me explaining my philosophy on why he couldn't go, and he understood." Douglas emphasized in his RF shoot that Corino called XPW first, not vice versa.

Additionally, despite reports that XPW lured him, GQ told me in September 2003 that "From what we were made to believe, Boogaloo got fired [by ROH] for considering working for us (when he wasn't who we were in contact with)," so XPW "[gave] him a job because he lost his other one due to us." A combination of his October 2002 "Diggin' Up Dirt Bert" column and his comments to me insisted that XPW received feelers of interest from at least six ROH and CZW talents (among them Boogaloo and Pain), two of whom "apparently [were] just stringing us along, saying they wanted to work for us when they really didn't."

Furthermore, GQ's 2003 account that "Justice Pain called our office continuously making the first contact" differs from Pain's November 2010 Yakuza Kick Radio claim that "they contacted me about four times and I said 'No, no, no'" and then they said 'What will it take to get you here?'" Either way, he named his own terms - an initial deposit (which almost all accounts say was $5,000) plus $600 guaranteed three times per month, regardless of whether XPW ran thrice.

On Yakuza Kick and in his subsequent SMV "Best on the Indies" shoot, Pain said he negotiated the deal with Kleinrock and that the initial money was used for a down-payment on a house. Pain told SMV that the first check for the house down-payment successfully cashed and only some of the subsequent checks cleared, but that XPW later gave him cash to make up for the bounced checks, and ultimately, he wasn't owed anything.

He recalled to SMV getting tire slash threats by e-mail, and elaborated on Yakuza Kick: "I actually got two death threats from people, and people telling me…'We know what you drive and your car's gonna be in flames and your tires are gonna be slashed and "f" your cunt girlfriend and we know who she is.'"

On Yakuza Kick, Pain said that there were talks of programming him against Douglas, while he told SMV thatTammy managing him in his feud with Candido was discussed. Douglas told me that "[Pain] claimed...that he wanted to come and was happy to be [in XPW]." Douglas says Pain, who passed away in 2020 told him, "It was time for me to leave [CZW]. I wasn't happy there anymore."

Contrary to popular belief, though, the talent poaching wasn't entirely one-sided. CZW negotiated with Luke and his trainer, Grimes, separately from one another. Additionally, Hamrick had recommended Youthanazia (Josh Prohibition & "M-Dogg 20" Matt Cross) to XPW before they were even in CZW.

According to GQ, meanwhile, there were some Philly era reports about XPW of questionable accuracy. For instance, Magee reported that "XPW called a ticket outlet for Philadelphia area independent 3PWrestling, claiming that 3PW was working with XPW in an attempt to get this outlet to sell XPW tickets." GQ dismissed that, saying "We were supposed to sell tickets at that comic book shop, but never under any false pretenses of working with 3PW." GQ said on May 1, 2008 on Rubber Guard Radio that Magee "was out to get us and expose anything he could."

The Philly period in-ring product was generally well received by XPW audiences. In his early 2003 PWNNV interview, Douglas specifically put over the January double-shot's success. However, he also admitted that "out of the six shows we've had [in Philly], we had one that I will tell you straight out sucked...just something was not right in the chemistry that night. I'm sure some of the ideas that I had come up with as the booker didn't produce well in the ring, some of the guys missed spots, just one of those nights where the sun and the moon and stars were lined up wrong." He mentioned on a November 25, 2002 Xtreme Mayhem Radio interview that Exit Sandman "didn't live up to our expectations" and that they "dropped the ball a little bit on" it, so likely he was referring to that show in the other interview as the Philly event that lacked in the typical quality.

Douglas gave me his opinions of CZW, ROH, and 3PW:

"The problem was the other promoters in the area were trying to get us from going in there...Anyone who's afraid of competition must be afraid of their product...[I'm] confident enough as a booker that if you can book better than me and outdraw me, then you got a better product. That's called 'extreme market system,' 'free enterprise.' So I had no problem with anybody else going into the building a day before if they asked us. Rob, however, saw it differently and wanted to try and get predatory...Those companies were all working to try to undermine us, they were trying to schedule shows opposite ours, to screw ours and we had no intent of going in there to hurt anybody. The weekend that we picked [for Hostile Takeover], we intentionally picked the first one to not run opposition to any of the other shows...I do distinctly remember talking about 'Find the dates out for CZW and 3PW and Ring of Honor to find out when they were running and to stay away from those.' Nevertheless, I don't know if they joined forces or what, but all three of them were doing shows against us."

On his podcast years later, Black didn't mention ROH, said he didn't care about 3PW, and gave varying accounts on CZW ranging from wanting to stick it to Zandig after being "egged on" about CZW to not having animosity toward it. Douglas admits that when the other companies became combative, his natural reaction was to become aggressive, too, advising PWNNV that "Anyone who knows Shane Douglas knows I won't shy away from a fight" and telling RF that "When someone tries to push us out of the market, we'll certainly push back."

Douglas advised Wrestling-News.com that he and Black had already faced some disagreements before Hostile Takeover, but worked them out:

"Rob Black and I have had some knock-down, drag-out arguments over content and where the show will go and where this company will go and the fact that I'm still with this company tells you that Rob Black has, where prudent, acquiesced and taken a step back and taken my advice...He's been good enough to listen...When he brings me up to speed on certain storylines, places where he disagrees with me and he won't back down, it makes sense that he doesn't back down for the history of the storyline."

That ability to cooperate changed as the Philly run progressed, Douglas told me:

"I don't wanna have to explain everything I'm doing, especially with something like wrestling that can become so convoluted and drawn out that it would take me hours and hours to explain why I'm doing something, especially with someone who doesn't understand the business."

Douglas further elaborated about the disagreements to RF Video:

"I would fight against [Rob] weekly on things...He would tell me his reasoning and I would give him three rebuttals to his reasoning and he would give me four more reasons and I'd give him four more rebuttals...[Wed' be] talking on the phone for three or four hours a night...After awhile, you say 'Hey, you know what? Do it your way, Rob.'"

At this point, when Douglas and Black started butting heads more frequently due to Douglas and Michaels "booking blindly from across the country in Pittsburgh" (Douglas' words to RF Video), the tide started to turn as far as XPW's perception among Pennsylvanians. Leaflets were even distributed to the local South Philadelphia neighborhood detailing XPW's porn connection. Anti-XPW buzz was abound when it announced "developmental" deals with Revolution Pro, FWA, and IWA Mid-South, which some saw as disrespectful to those already respected organizations. XPW attendance in Philly started strong, but slipped to, by one account, less than 75 during the second half of a Valentine's Day 2003 show that was main evented by one of the best matches in company history, Juventud Guerrera vs. Jonny Storm. The same month, it lost TV in Philly for failure to pay for its time slot.

XPW leasing the ECW Arena also turned out to be futile. According to two sources, it was paying $8,000 monthly to prevent other promotions from running there. Zandig added on Yakuza Kick that XPW's initial $60,000 security deposit bounced. Douglas told me he was "deadset against [the lease] because to me it didn't make any sense for that kind of money," and GQ called it "the biggest waste of money" on Xtreme Memories. Douglas recalled to RF warning Black to "beat [competitors] on your product, but don't try to beat them at the game" because to "corner the market" by preventing "anybody from running in this building" could result in "alienating the fans." Nonetheless, Douglas said that the "outlandishly crazy" deal Black did "behind my back...became an albatross around the neck of XPW" public relations-wise because Black ignored his advice and exercised the exclusivity clause. On February 28, XPW lost its lease to the Arena due to bounced checks, which some talent were also receiving.

With attendance shrinking in Philly, XPW returned to California on February 28 and March 1 with perhaps its two best shows ever, wrestling-wise. However, Douglas told RF that despite California management hyping it up, the paintball venue, which had paint chips dropping from the ceiling, "was without a doubt the worst building I've ever laid eyes on." Veronica indicated less than a month later in her XMR interview that from what she heard about the X-Park weekend, "They had nobody to set up their stuff. So, every single person that had a pair of hands had to show up [to work]...because they've been gone from LA and they've burned so many bridges that they didn't have a ring crew." Borden was even said to be sweeping up paintball debris and told a fan that XPW would never return to that venue.

It was this California weekend that Tom Byron fan Sean Waltman (X-Pac) debuted in-ring for XPW. GQ says he "was living in LA, so he went into the office late one night" and filmed a vignette challenging Kaos for the TV title. There was an incident between the two after that match, GQ told me:

"Pac confronted Kaos because I guess Kaos stiffed him pretty good...It was definitely professional, but Pac talked about how next week in Pittsburgh we should bring it from the heart, and take our emotions into the ring 'because that makes for the best matches' and that was fine. Problem was he never showed up. That's where our heat came from. I mean, we dropped the strap...but then, the guy had the nerve to no-show, which in fact, he had a reputation of doing."

GQ elaborated in a Casa D-18 Studios interview in late 2011, saying Waltman "came to the show [that he wrestled Kaos on] high as hell wearing Chyna's pants and...there was a shoving match in the back. A lot of yelling and screaming." Waltman admitted on a November 10, 2010 Awesome Bomb Fight Radio interview that he wasn't entirely professional while in XPW:

"I was pretty fucked up back [during my XPW run]. Here's how I knew that 'OK, this is the place that I was supposed to be at right now.' I showed up three hours late, and I still wasn't even the last one of the boys to get there, and the people were just sitting there waiting, not even mad because they already knew that's how that place ran."

GQ specified in the Casa D-18 Studios interview that "It wasn't that Kaos had issues with dropping the belt; it was Kaos had issues dropping the belt to X-Pac, a guy who we knew would be unreliable." GQ added that the costume he dressed up in in Pittsburgh to mock Waltman was so believable that Credible mistook him for Waltman from behind. In Waltman's defense, Douglas told me he had warned management that he'd probably be arriving late due to a tight flight. Waltman said on In Your Head in April 2010 that he liked Kaos and that after finding his XPW championship belt in his mother's attic years later, he donated it to charity.

GQ mentioned to Casa D-18 Studios that around the time of the Pittsburgh event, "The writing was on the wall that XPW was dying." On March 11, XPWrestling.com announced GQ, Kaos, and GQ's then-girlfriend J-Love as being "released...from their commitments." GQ explained to me, "When we got back from Pittsburgh, I had talked with Kevin. The Monday when we got home (March 10) was my last day with the company." As far as Kaos and J-Love, he says, "Honestly, I did something I shouldn't have done, and I spoke on their behalf. I do know that

Kaos did have his own meeting with Rob and Kevin, though." GQ advised Casa D-18 Studios that Black fired him by e-mail, "which was fine because at that point I was quitting as well. Fired technically, which is great because it allowed me to get unemployment." Kaos recalled a few years later, "I was fired from XPW thru the web site along with GQ. No call. Nothing. I negotiated to come back without GQ."

The Pittsburgh show's success, which was partially due to Douglas' local roots generating article into community newspapers days before the show, led to investigation into promoting events in new markets like Cleveland, Florida, and New York City. However, none of those prospects were to be. Also, an April 19 Pittsburgh return was prematurely cancelled by the California management for unclear reasons, without consulting Douglas. On a 2004 Interactive Interview podcast, Douglas said that as a result of Black suddenly wanting to un-cancel upon hearing how well its tickets were selling, "I said [to Black] 'You can't un-cancel a canceled show. You can't create that kind of confusion in the marketplace." Douglas said on The Interactive Interview that it was at this point that he decided to "tap out" as it pertained to XPW.

Douglas has also said in interviews that XPW stopped excelling in storyline consistency and TV production quality, making his words in his Wrestling-News.com interview leading into his first show in charge seem ominous: "[In ECW], we offered them a product the fans could buy into and they could consistently trust and that's what this company XPW will do under me, or I'll leave it. It'll live up to every bit of a standard that I set in ECW, or I'll walk away from it." Instead of his Wrestling-News.com prediction that "in the next 6-8 months" XPW would become "a company that runs 6-8 times every month" coming true, XPW hit roadblock after roadblock. Later in that interview, Douglas said, "One thing I am certain of - XPW will make further mistakes. As we make them, that's not to say to flush us down the toilet. We're gonna learn by it. We're gonna grow by it. It's exactly the same process ECW went through." All of that is exactly what happened - XPW made mistakes, learned some lessons along the way, and eventually stopped offering fans a consistent product, and Douglas departed it as he warned would happen if the product delivery fell short.

After Douglas quit the company out of frustration, matters got worse--far worse, in fact. On April 8, exactly one month after the Pittsburgh show, Extreme Associates' office was raided for federal obscenity-related matters. Pittsburgh was not only the most financially profitable show in the company's history, attracting 1,500 paid customers with only 30-40 comped tickets, according to Douglas' RF shoot; it also was the final show of XPW's original incarnation.

Black, Kleinrock, nor anyone else ever made an official announcement about XPW closing doors. Byron wrote in an October 10, 2003 post on AdultDVDTalk.com that XPW "is in sort of hiatus right now. Its future will depend on the numbers on the next couple of pay-per-views for InDemand and DirectTV." XPW quietly faded out of business, a stark contrast to the boastful newspaper ads and RSPW threads hyping its launch. There would be XPW reunion shows years later, but the homegrown crew never got the opportunity to close the book on the promotion in a proper way during its original run.

Several non-wrestlers - Black, Borden, Byron, Kleinrock, Kloss, and Hernandez - remained the entire run as a part of the company. Kaos and Supreme were the wrestlers who lasted the entire length of live events, and Supreme was the only grappler who never left.

On the August 25, 2014 "Kris Kloss Show" podcast, Kloss, who said on Xtreme Memories that an XPW fan recognized him at the Roman Colosseum years later, eloquently articulated XPW's effect on those previously inexperienced So-Cal talents whose lives it impacted:

"We were very young at that time, and we want to prove ourselves...We were on television doing what we love. It just couldn't get any better...For everybody that went off to college, brother, [XPW] was my college. That was our fucking college or fraternity, dude...and I would never trade that in for going to a regular college because how many fucking people in this country - hundreds and millions and whatever - go to college? How many fucking people go to a wrestling company, be on TV, go into a porn studio every week?"

After XPW folded, the XPW decision makers made up with most of the power players who opposed them during the Philly wars. GQ became Facebook friends with Feinstein and former-3PW co-promoters Blue Meanie and Tod Gordon. He even has been seen interacting on social media with ex-CZW commentator and part-time booker Eric Gargiulo, who had written in an April 17, 2003 ProWrestlingRadio.com column that GQ getting legitimately hurt by a punch from Messiah at a post-attack indie show was deserved. Furthermore, GQ served as a guest instructor at a 2019 EVOLVE seminar of former-ROH booker Gabe Sapolsky.

Douglas, meanwhile, did shoot interviews in 2003 and 2005 with Feinstein's RF Video company. Sapolsky used Douglas for an in-ring promo at a June 12, 2005 ROH show and did a shoot interview with him and Funk for ROH the same weekend. Douglas also reunited with Meanie and Gordon on ECW reunion shows that happened post-XPW.

Kleinrock collaborated with Sapolsky's Dragon Gate USA promotion for a 2010 Bob Saget TV show episode and worked closely with Meanie in Extreme Rising. The post-XPW distribution company Kleinrock was Executive Vice President for, Big Vision Entertainment, licensed footage from CZW during the Zandig era, and Kleinrock recalled in 2020 that he thinks, but isn't certain, that he had conversations directly with Zandig. Big Vision also licensed Feinstein's shoot interviews footage for two of its DVDs. Additionally, Kleinrock became Facebook friends with Feinstein, Gargiulo, and Gordon.

Then, of course, there's Black and Borden. In the 2010s, Borden became avid social media pals with Meanie. She took pictures with him at conventions, as well as one with Feinstein. Likewise, both Black and Borden seemed to have made up on social media in the same decade with 3PW's Jasmin, who they had developed tension with in Extreme Associates and XPW around the turn of the century. Black also had talks with Feinstein about doing a shoot interview that never came to fruition, but he is not believed to have ever had post-XPW contact with Gargiulo, Sapolsky, Zandig, or Meanie. So, the majority of the Philly indie wars era wounds were healed post-XPW, with some exceptions.

Likewise, former-XPW personalities had their ups and downs in the decades that followed. WSX aired on MTV in 2007 and featured many XPW alumni working alongside CZW stars. Messiah, Supreme, and other XPW wrestlers starred in a backyard wrestling video game. Dynamite D, Kristian Blood, Big Rott, Supreme, and Felony passed away. Grimes became a motorcycle minister, Myst an inventor, and GQ a full-time WWE backstage employee, as Funk suggested should happen in his autobiography. Lazie's engagement to and subsequent split from *The Big Bang Theory* TV star Kaley Cuoco got mainstream press. Darlin beat cervical cancer. After failed CZW negotiations during XPW's existence, Kaos and Luke both ended up having stays in CZW, did extra work for WWE, and launched their own training schools, and Luke did stunt work in movies alongside Dwayne "The Rock" Johnson and other A-list actors. Kloss performed on Broadway for the play "Alice In Wonderland." Black and Borden went to federal prison for the obscenity charges for a little less than a year each, before they separated. Both left porn, with Black returning to wrestling for a few shows and then moving back to Rochester, having two sons, and opening a restaurant with Byron.

XPW was dead, and like it or not, life went on for everyone.

11. Speaking From Experience

I started writing this book in the year XPW folded, 2003. In 2007 at Ursinus College, I heard about a CHIKARA show taking place on campus. I knew that CHIKARA had run a show at Ursinus in 2005, but had assumed it was just a chance happening. I went to the campus activities office and was told to contact a particular student about assisting with the show. From her last name, I instantly put two and two together and realized that she was the sister of indie mainstay and CHIKARA patriarch Mike Quackenbush. I excitedly e-mailed her as well as Mike and arrived at the indoor fieldhouse venue the next day hours before the show's start time. I met the ring crew as they arrived, then Mike's sister, and finally Mike. I told Mike that I was aware that Bryce, the senior referee, had both officiated and ring announced the previous Ursinus show. I asked if I could ring announce this show. Mike approved that request, and I did.

When I officially joined the company as a ref in training later that year, Mike gave me a choice - either write about wrestling or train in it. I couldn't continue writing about XPW. I, without hesitation, picked the latter option, wanting to prove to myself and others that I could do more in wrestling than just write about it. Debuting in-ring in 2008, I lasted with the company until it folded in 2020.

Each CHIKARA show at the ECW Arena, Pennsylvania State Athletic Commission representative Frank Talent, who had been the inspector assigned to XPW's Philly shows, would introduce me to the show's doctor. The elder Talent's memory was starting to go by this time and the doctor and I always played along, acting like we were meeting each other for the first time.

Joey Styles commentated over five of my matches during his brief CHIKARA stint. I refereed singles matches of former-XPW stars Sabu, Sean Waltman, and Justin Credible. Sabu came across backstage as a totally unprofessional bully, while Waltman asked me for weed. As I don't smoke, I didn't have any, although I pointed him in the right direction of who to talk to. When I reffed Waltman, I think he got blown up quickly because what was supposed to be a regular match ended up only going four minutes. I literally met Credible in the ring, as traffic being a bear caused me to arrive right as his match was starting.

At a TNA show in September 2010, I was asked backstage to relay a message to Bubba Ray Dudley. He was talking to Angelina Love, so I stood by and waited a half minute until they were done conversing so that I didn't interrupt, and then gave Bubba the communication. Apparently, I cockblocked his Angelina pursuit because he, apparently frustrated, asked "Can't you see I'm trying to get laid?" Angelina grimaced at that.

In 2005, I was interviewing Jerry Lynn for this book and had to call him back twice after the initial interview was done because I forgot to ask certain questions. After that, TNA had the wrestler call me rather than me call them when I interviewed talent. Not surprising. Five years later, my trainer Claudio Castagnoli (WWE's Cesaro) told me a few days before an ROH show I would be doing ring crew at that Lynn was going to be inducted into the ECW Arena Hardcore Hall Of Fame. So, I approached Lynn before the ROH show and inquired about who was going to induct him into the hall of fame hours later. Lynn asked me twice what I was talking about before I said "Nevermind," thinking maybe I was mistaken. During that night's show, Jim Cornette came out, introduced him, and inducted him as what was supposed to be a surprise to him. So, I spoiled for Lynn his hall of fame induction. Oops!

Then there's Tommy Dreamer, who you may remember commented on XPW earlier in this book. In 2006, I wanted to acquire Dreamer's story of *Whack Attack 5* and his opinion on XPW. I set up an interview with him through a promoter for after a show, but when he asked what the interview would be about and I said "XPW," he responded "not interested" and walked away.

I didn't give up. In addition to wanting his participation in this book, my teenage self also had the delusion that I was going to be the first person to do a shoot interview with Dreamer, despite not knowing the first thing about cameras. I called his cell phone. When we connected, he told me that contrary to what he read on the Internet, he hadn't blown me off. He absolutely had, of course, and the only place I wrote that he blew me off was legendary gossip sleaze site DOIWrestling.com, which meant that Dreamer was a DOI reader. I got a kick out of that.

We discussed his *Whack Attack 5* cameo. Dreamer indicated interest in locating a copy of the film. I directed him to a search engine and instructed what query to type in, and he proceeded to recite what he'd find. Think "The Innovator Of Violence" reading about porn in a dull, monotone voice: "Ashlyn Gere sucks Tom Byron's dick until she's covered in cum," and similar sentences. Dreamer apparently was in front of a computer while I wasn't, and was just going off of what I was telling him. I'd say "Click on this. Scroll. Now click on that." At one point when we were having some trouble finding this pornographic film, he proceeded to indicate to me slight disappointment in me for my lousy directions.

Eventually, after he looked for several minutes on the Internet, he indicated that he had found it, and seemed satisfied. I have no idea whether he purchased it. I was barely of legal age to buy porn when this conversation took place. Many people have probably heard Dreamer utter the word "buffet," but I'm confident that I'm the only person to ever hear him directly precede it with the word "butthole."

That following Monday, I belatedly listened to my cell phone messages and noticed one from Dreamer:

"This is Tommy Dreamer calling for Jonathan...[pause] I don't know how to pronounce the last name. Call me back at your convenience. I don't know if I'll be able to do an interview, but I'll be happy to speak to you."

My last name is "Barber," of course.

Fast forward a few years to Dreamer's CHIKARA appearances, the first times I had seen or talked to him since 2006. At King Of Trios 2012, I reffed him, Lynn, & 2 Cold Scorpio vs. Mike Bennett & The Young Bucks. After we got backstage, Dreamer said in a loud, emphatic voice, "Where's our referee?!" I went up to him and gulped, "That's me." He looked at me for a few seconds and then said "You're one hell of a ref. Great job! GREAT JOB!" I was so relieved. Then Lynn came right up to me, shook my hand, and thanked me. I went over to Scorpio, who I was nervous to thank because I thought I'd get criticism from him, given that he'd criticized the far more experienced Bryce the previous night. Scorpio thanked me, too, and didn't give me any critique. I was on top of the world that night. This is one of the matches I'm most proud of.

While in CHIKARA, I also met Gary Yap, the promoter of XPW's cross-town rival EPIC. The first time I AIMed Gary, he, without me identifying myself, knew exactly who I was, writing "Hey Barber." He later drove cross country with Tony Kozina and the future-Simon Gotch to King Of Trios 2009. The first time I encountered Gary was backstage. He was carrying some boxes and we awkwardly made small talk as he tried to keep hold of them. EPIC co-promoter Anthony Maris a few months later tweeted something like "@TDonst: "When Gary and Barber met, it was like Hogan and The Rock shaking hands." Classic. Tim Donst was a CHIKARA wrestler who was also making his name at the time in So-Cal for Gary's promotion. The next morning, Gary and I talked more substantively. That weekend, he tweeted something along the lines of, "Just had a great conversation with Jon Barber. He's a good guy, unlike what some people say about him."

At Trios, I also had a substantive conversation with Kozina about So-Cal wrestling and our mutual friend Rizzono. At the end of the weekend as he was leaving, Gotch approached me. We had this exchange:

GOTCH: "Hey, are you Jon Barber?"

ME: "Yes."

GOTCH: "*The* Jon Barber?"

ME: "Yes."

GOTCH: (after staring at me in silence for several seconds, in a very serious voice) "I knocked out Pogo The Clown."

ME: "...OK."

One XPW talent who wasn't supportive of this book was Johnny Webb. By reffing in nearly half of the U.S. states on someone else's dime, I accomplished more geographically-speaking. I will say that Webb has my respect for working his tail off to produce most of the XPW TV show. That being said, I'm not the only person to say that he has a difficult personality to mesh with, as a few XPW personalities (including Pogo) told me the same thing, mentioning without prompting from me that they didn't like him.

While Webb did get a paycheck from wrestling outside of the ring like I do, he did so while working 18 hour days that by his own admission were split between editing the XPW TV show and splicing bukkake porn, and in total he worked for two major companies, XPW and WSX, for less than five years total. I have spent about 15 years and counting earning wrestling behind-the-scenes consulting money from a total of about 10 major indie wrestling companies without having to leave my house and making my own hours. I may not even have gotten involved in my current wrestling consulting work if it wasn't for Kleinrock, as he asked me around 2005 if I could assist him behind-the-scenes with Big Vision, so I trace my current consulting success back to XPW.

Through XPW, I got more free merchandise (Big Vision Entertainment's screeners list, and more), gained more business associates (i.e. Kevin Kleinrock) and acquaintances (Vic Grimes, GQ Money, etc.), and struck up more friendships (including Verne Langdon, Dynamite D, Mark "Guido" Mancini, David "Shooting Star" Floridia," Rizzono, and two fellow XPW fans) than many other people ever did. I milked XPW for everything it was worth, and still do to this day. That doesn't mean I don't appreciate what I got and get out of it. I absolutely do, but I've also used my experience XPW to grow as a person and for that, I am thankful.

I mentioned Kleinrock above. I worked for Kevin at Extreme Rising and the Urban Wrestling Federation (UWF). I had never met him in person when I walked into the Hammerstein Ballroom in June 2011. He told me I'd be shadowing UWF (and former-XPW Philly) producer Cody Michaels as an assistant. Before I could even be introduced to Cody, I (aware he was a Pittsburgh native) pinpointed exactly who he was by the Pirates jersey he was wearing.

I also worked the December UWF tapings. While I certainly wasn't, I felt like a true journeyman wrestling referee because I reffed on three straight days of CHIKARA JoshiMania shows in Philly, then Massachusetts, and finally Manhattan. Instead of going home after the New York City show, I stayed over at a CHIKARA wrestler's home in the Bronx and took public transportation into Manhattan again for the first of two consecutive UWF taping days. The second of those days (Tuesday), I ran into Atlas Security's Ronnie Lang, who I had seen four days earlier in Philly when he serviced CHIKARA's ECW Arena show. Lang was freshly rested, while I was a zombie, having been on the road for five straight days. However, as I was paid to sit among ringside strippers and hold a microphone during the show in return for my best payday ever (triple digits for those minimal production duties), I wasn't going to complain.

I remember seeing Kevin getting aggressively screamed at in the face by his UWF boss and Rob Black adversary Steve Karel. I was rooting for him, thinking to myself "Yell back, Kevin!" Finally, he did, screaming in Karel's face even louder than Karel had yelled at him. Yay! I was so impressed. I've always enjoyed interacting with Kevin.

Another person I can't praise enough is Dynamite D. Darren saw the good in me even when I was a dumb teenager who screwed up often. I was heartbroken when he passed away from cancer in April 2007. I wrote and posted online a remembrance about him. I never sent my Darren tribute to Dave Meltzer or any of his writers, but somehow, the Wrestling Observer web site picked it up.

At Ursinus' Relay For Life cancer research fundraiser that took place a few days after Darren passed, I went up to the tech guy when I noticed that students were getting names of loved ones who passed from cancer aired on the mega screen. I asked him to add a slide that read "Darren 'Dynamite D' McMillan." I must have then stared at that screen for 10 straight minutes, waiting for Darren's name to appear after all the others. It eventually did. At that moment, I looked up to the heavens and smiled. That was for you, D.

Another XPW personality I interacted with was Lizzy Borden. I started talking to her through MySpace in 2007. In May 2008, she came to Philadelphia for a strip club show. Teenage me originally became a fan of XPW for two reasons, Kristi Myst and Lizzy Borden, and I ended up basically living my dream to a degree with Lizzy in Philly. She walked off stage in the middle of her performance, came over to me, and said "You're Jonathan, right?" I said "Yes." Later that night, I asked her how she knew my name before I could introduce myself and she said that she recognized me from my MySpace photo.

She directed me to the VIP lounge. There, she asked "You know Robert, right?" I couldn't hear her over the loud music. She repeated it, but I still couldn't hear her. Finally, at the top of her lungs, she shouted in my ear, "I said, 'You know Robert, right?!'" She turned her head in the direction of an individual sitting in the corner of the dark room, wearing all black and with a baseball cap covering his face. I had noticed him when I walked in, but didn't think anything of him. She had shouted it so loud that that person heard what she said. At that moment, for a few seconds, time stopped. As my face panned horizontally to the side, towards the figure, this figure's head lifted vertically up, and our eyes met.

It was Rob Black in the flesh! My jaw dropped and I was silent for a few seconds before exclaiming, "Rob, how the fuck are you?" He said no words at first, instead unleashing his Rochester hyena-style cackle of a laugh. Then, he uttered "How are ya, kid?!" At that point, I abandoned Lizzy for most of the rest of the night and interacted with Rob. I took a photo with them. She was charging anyone else who wanted a photo, but she insisted I not pay and told me it was free. At the bottom of the photo, which they both signed, she wrote "Loved it!" I got out of that club in the early morning, slept in my car in a nearby parking lot, and drove straight to the ECW Arena early Saturday morning to meet some CHIKARA staff members to drive to Massachusetts for a show. So, this was my XPW "cold day in hell," and it took place while XPW alumni were gearing up for the following night's reunion show over 2,500 miles away in Redondo Beach.

With Rob Black & Lizzy Borden. From author's personal photo collection.

I kept in touch with Lizzy via social media on occasion. When Hulk Hogan's agent Peter Young approached Kleinrock about doing a reality TV project with Rob and Lizzy shortly before they entered prison, it was me who passed Young's contact info along, not Kleinrock, who had some heat with Rob and Lizzy at the time. While she was in prison, I received a hand-written letter from Lizzy that ended with "Gotta go now. Time for the four o'clock count." I also talked to Rob's mom on social media a few times. She responded to one of my facebook posts and we started conversing late one night, and kept in touch for a while.

Rob and Lizzy's attorney in their obscenity case was Louis Sirkin, who also represented Larry Flynt and plenty of other defendants in landmark similar trials and is probably the most respected First Amendment attorney in the U.S. While I can't confirm that it's true, Rob or Lizzy have claimed that just to get Sirkin on the phone to be able to say "Hi, we're facing 50 years in prison for obscenity charges and were wondering if you can assist us?" cost a $15,000 consultation fee. I met and worked with Sirkin at a censorship symposium in Pennsylvania, I went out to dinner (on someone else's dime) at a fancy restaurant with him and four or five other people and picked his brain about First Amendment issues that night, as well as the following day.

With Rob Black and Lizzy Borden's lawyer, Louis Sirkin (April 9, 2010). From author's personal photo collection.

I also enjoyed my interactions with Chris Hamrick. In 2003, I was actually the first person I know of to get an on-the-record interview with him about his two week relationship with Kristi Myst. Later, around 2006 during the MySpace days, I was in touch with Myst, and Hamrick found out and asked me to put him back in touch with her. When I tried to, she didn't seem eager to talk to him again. Sometimes, reunions aren't all they're cracked up to be. Hamrick frequently mentions in interviews that the highlight of his wrestling career was Kristi Myst, and the highlight of mine was my encounter with Borden, so we kind of have that in common, I guess. On second thought, I take that back–maybe the highlight of my career was touring China, which Hamrick and I also share the experience of. In fact, in 2014 I again talked to Hamrick, asking him what to expect in China. While he wrote to me that "the food sucks" and "they have prostitution," at least on the food front, China was the total opposite of his description, as we at WWN were fed like royalty.

In addition to reffing for CHIKARA and WWN, you could also say I crossed the line and betrayed XPW (ha!) by reffing and working ring crew for their enemy, CZW. In fact, there was a short period where I considered CZW more my home than CHIKARA, as I would see the CZW crew several times weekly and only saw the CHIKARA roster twice a month. Then-CZW owner DJ Hyde even said once during a post-show tirade to the roster something like "JB is a CHIKARA guy and he is here more often and works harder than most of you." Other times, DJ joked with me about a Kaos t-shirt I was wearing and about Bubba Ray Dudley's skills as a porn director; surprisingly, he already knew about Bubba's alternate career without me mentioning it to him.

Quackenbush also teased me about an XPW t-shirt I was wearing, this time of Pogo. As we were holding wall-sit squats during training, each person named their favorite wrestler, and Mike said "Pogo The Clown." Another time that we were also doing wall-sits, I named "Chris Hamrick" as my favorite and when the exercise was over, Claudio jokingly uttered "Who said Chris

Hamrick?" I later recounted that story on twitter to Claudio while he was in WWE and he tweeted back "#hamrickbump."

During my reffing days, though, I was largely out of the XPW loop. I sold most of my XPW merchandise and barely thought about it for over 10 years. CHIKARA and whatever other promotions I was working for were my focus. Then Conrad, the person who ended up designing the cover for this book, got in touch with me. He had passion for XPW, like I used to years before. When my mom ended up in the hospital and I found myself sitting at her bedside for weeks at a time in 2018, I thought to myself that I should do something with all that I wrote about XPW years before. By then, it was a different era than when I started training in 2007. Wrestling personalities could write for the public now. I was no longer bound to Quackenbush's ultimatum to either work or write. I had everything I had written about XPW saved, so, being influenced by Conrad's XPW ardor, I started working on this book again, including conducting interviews. It's through that work that this book came to be.

Just as XPW wouldn't have been what it was without Verne Langdon, this book also wouldn't be what it is without Verne. He became a friend of my family and a mentor of mine. At least two people have told me how highly Verne thought of and talked about me to them, which is an honor, as I tremendously respect the man. I wrote about him in a tribute a week after he passed. As was also the case with the Darren tribute, it was the most eloquent way I could convey what Verne meant to me. I recommend giving both a read.

I never told Verne that I became a referee. In the months that lead up to his passing, I kept telling myself that I should e-mail Verne and update him on how I was doing, but I never did. I even thought of him a week before he passed and again procrastinated from contacting him. Then, one day in early January 2011, I signed onto the SCU message board and saw a thread titled "Verne Langdon." I excitedly clicked on it, assuming people would be talking about Verne and Slammers' influence on So-Cal wrestling. I was shocked to read "R.I.P." I realized at that moment that you should never procrastinate from telling people you care about what they mean to you because you may not get another opportunity. I kept putting Verne off and the opportunity to catch up with him passed me by.

That being said, I have wonderful memories of Verne. This is despite me ignoring his advice many times, as a stupid teenager. This was the case in June 2007, when after we had a minor disagreement, he wrote to me that he still supported me. Besides signing his name, the very last words Verne ever wrote to me came in that e-mail: "Believe it or not, I'm on YOUR side!"

Without a shadow of a doubt, he was indeed.

Sources:

XPW/IWA http://www.pwbts.com/columns/b020403.html

Diggin Up Dirt Bert on ROH:
https://web.archive.org/web/20021008084833/http://www.1wrestling.com:80/news/newsline.asp?news=10755

Lukeford http://www.socaluncensored.com/board/forum/wrestling/southern-california-wrestling-forum/1225-xpw-problems-lukeford-com

Went through 2002 threads which end at
http://www.socaluncensored.com/board/forum/wrestling/southern-california-wrestling-forum/page533

https://web.archive.org/web/20011103151726/http://www.xpw1.com:80/messages/12.shtml

https://web.archive.org/web/20010620105808/http://www.xpw1.com:80/messages/121.html

https://web.archive.org/web/20010424213921/http://www.xpw1.com:80/messages/16.html

http://www.socaluncensored.com/board/forum/wrestling/southern-california-wrestling-forum/2346-rev-pro-becomes-an-xpw-developmental-territory developmental territories

http://www.socaluncensored.com/board/forum/wrestling/southern-california-wrestling-forum/2627-it-s-official-kaos-mystery-opponent-is-xpac x-pac/byron

http://www.socaluncensored.com/board/forum/wrestling/southern-california-wrestling-forum/2758-xpw-cancel-4-4-4-5-shows-in-l-a

Thank You:

All of the people who granted interviews
Steve Bryant & SoCalUncensored.com
Art Heinrich
"Boxcar Josh"/Timmy Reed
Chris Hughes
Edgar Arce ("El Toro Bravo"), owner of Slammers Wrestling Gym and Slam U University
GQ Money
Highspots
K. Dawn Langdon, Esq., Atty. for Estate of Verne Langdon
Kayfabe Commentaries
Ken O'Neill
Kevin Kleinrock
Joe LaChance
Joel Gertner
Kayfabe Commentaries
RF Video
Smart Mark Video
Verne Langdon
The Wayback Machine/Archive.org
Whitney Hinton (TNA/Impact Wrestling)

THE HISTORY OF SHOOT INTERVIEWS

7.   The interviewee's experience

8.   Alternatives to the traditional shoot interview (Wrestling personalities-hosted shows/Shoot interviews with live audiences/Podcasts)

9.   Bootlegging & Piracy

The conception of shoot interviews

The idea for a pro wrestler to talk about their career is different from mainstream news interviews with celebrities about their own careers - which have been happening on talk shows and late night shows for many decades - only insofar as wrestling was more protected for years than mainstream entertainment was. Wrestlers could do promos all day long in the '80s. However, due to the restrictions of kayfabe, to ask them to do the same thing--talk--outside of storyline back then was virtually unheard of because wrestlers were expected to not break character. As Sean Oliver, the co-founder of shoot-style programming company Kayfabe Commentaries, said in an Insiders Edge Podcast in May 2021 that at one time, "the old-timers...were the guys who had to fight in the bars to preserve the integrity of the illusion, so to hear them come out" in rare, non-kayfabe interviews and openly discuss how wrestling worked behind-the-scenes was really something special.

Michael Bochicchio, the owner of long-time shoot interviews producer Highspots, said in a January 2004 SLAM! Wrestling article that doing "these types of interviews" is a next step that "naturally follows" from "the average fan wanting to know more about the business." As kayfabe has become more open, wrestling fans are as curious about the personal lives and views of wrestling personalities as Hollywood fans are about mainstream celebrities. Shoot interviews show wrestling figures as real people, just like tell-all TV interviews depict the fascinating true lives of A-list actors and actresses.

As Oliver said in a 2017 In Your Head interview, "That's why TMZ is popular, and all those kind of shows, because people want a peek inside something they're not supposed to see. I guess we'll all voyeurs at heart." It is no different than Hollywood gossip news magazines that portray the good and bad of the daily functionings mainstream famous people; some fans of movies and TV don't care about the personal life of, for instance, Tom Hanks, and prefer simply to enjoy his contributions through Forrest Gump, Cast Away, and Captain Phillips. Similarly, some wrestling fans only want to watch in-ring content and backstage skits that set up that in-ring content, and shoot interviews usually don't include live matches, which is (along with promos and vignettes) the main drawing point for a wrestling program. This is to say that there are certainly fans out there who prefer to let their fandom of Terry Funk blossom through watching his on-screen feuds with the likes of Jerry "The King" Lawler, Ric Flair, and Mick Foley. That being said, there are also those fans who prefer to go behind the curtain to get the true Terry Funk experience. For the latter, Funk has granted more than 10 shoot interviews that take fans behind the curtain.

Oliver was right when he told Luke Winkie of Deadspin in June 2019 that not all wrestling fans are a part of the shoot interview demographic. Oliver explains who the market is for shoot interviews:

"It's not even the wrestling fan. It's the wrestling fan that's interested in the business of wrestling. Then it's the wrestling fan that's interested in the business of wrestling enough to listen to someone talk about it for three hours."

Although the first instance of the phrase "shoot interview" being typed on Google Group rec.sport.pro-wrestling (RSPW) is from October 15, 1993, one of the first (if not the very first) shoot interview with a wrestler occurred in the '80s. It was with Bruiser Brody and took place shortly before his death. It was aired on a local

TV channel in Virginia back in the '80s, and although the 20 minute raw footage had been seen by a lot of people on YouTube, little was known about the behind-the-scenes wranglings of the interview until April 21, 2014, when John Corrigan, a wrestling journalist and at the time a Temple University student, published an article on the interview's background in the weekly Temple News newspaper. Corrigan equated Brody divulging his real name "within the first three minutes of the video" with the commission of "sacrilege" by '80s wrestling terms.

In the article, titled Bruiser Brody's 'Shoot Interviewer' revealed, Corrigan imparted that it was actually his uncle, who wished to remain anonymous, who had conducted the classic out of character interview with Brody. Corrigan's uncle was quoted in the article as saying, "It was my first job. I was a weekend sports anchor/weekday reporter and photographer for a small NBC affiliate in southern West Virginia." Of his impressions of Brody, the interviewer told his nephew, "He blew me away with how articulate he was. I was impressed with his depth as a person, as well as his depth as a character."

Another early shoot interview, and the first circulated shoot interview conducted in the traditional hotel setting, was one that Bob Barnett conducted with Eddie Gilbert in mid-1993 in a Ramada Inn room in Jackson, TN, called "Looking For Mr. Gilbert." It lasted a little over one and three quarter hours and the timeline jumped in it, as some events were not discussed in chronological order. Gilbert died less than two years after the interview was shot.

Feinstein has said in a Wrestling with the Future interview that he saw the Gilbert shoot and "thought it was horribly shot" and "was like 'I can do this.'" Feinstein hyped a shoot interview (which he didn't conduct) with Abdullah The Butcher at Abby's Atlanta restaurant on RSPW on June 2, 1996, and he also has repeatedly credited Wade Keller's Torch Talk interviews in the mid-90s as inspiration for his shoots. He said on the Duke Loves Rasslin Week 191 podcast that he thought to himself, "'Why is nobody doing these on video?' So, I started doing them on video, and we started doing the ECW guys first."

Having built-in connections with and access to ECW talent was, in fact, one of the benefits of handling ECW's videography at the time. In fact, while Feinstein has never been certain when asked who the first RF Video shoot interview was with, it had to have been with someone from ECW, and not surprisingly, the six names that have been thrown around as possibilities for the first one are from ECW - Sandman, Tommy Rich, New Jack, and Louie Spicolli. Some evidence points to New Jack as being the first, as his first interview took place at the end of 1996, after November 23's Mass Transit incident, but being that nobody seems to know for sure, it is certainly not confirmed that New Jack launched the series.

Of course, the early RF interviews did not have very advanced production value; the intro for the Rob Van Dam shoot to this day reads "Ron Van Dam." RF Video employee Eric Gargiulo conducted most of the early editions of RF shoots; Feinstein said on the Wrestling with the Future podcast that this was "because I just felt nervous one-on-one with the guys looking at them." The early shoots took place in the RF Video office, often with the subject sitting on a couch. According to Feinstein's words on Roundtable Wrestling Radio on January 11, 2010, "word of mouth" among those in the wrestling brotherhood led to other personalities trusting him, and consequently he was able to expand to non-ECW wrestlers for shoot interviews, and his shoot interviews business grew.

Thanks to both its official business relationship with ECW and other promotions' lax copyright policies during the late '90s, RF would sometimes include "b-roll" stock footage on its shoots. If a wrestler was asked about a specific match or promo, RF sometimes aired that match or promo before or after the part of the shoot where they talked about it. As RF began marketing its ECW archive on separate DVDs and Japanese promotions, WWE, etc. cracked down on copyright infringement in subsequent years, RF took most or all of that b-roll footage out of their shoots, re-released them, and restricted the content of its future shoot videos strictly to the sit-down portions with the respective personalities.

Highspots got started in the shoot interviews market in 1998, about two years after RF Video, and at first it sold only four shoot interviews. Three were Smoky Mountain Wrestling (SMW) Fanweek interviews from 1993-1995 that they didn't conduct, each with Jim Cornette, and the fourth was the first shoot Highspots ever conducted, which was with Ricky Morton in 1998. As time went on, Highspots conducted more interviews after Morton, but as they've gone on the record about in the product description of the Vampiro: Another Nail in the Coffin shoot in the late 2000s, they were, in the early 2000s, "struggling in the shoot interview market. That was until Michael sat down and turned on the camera on Vampiro." That first Vampiro shoot in 2002 was extremely candid and saw him shoot hard on Rob Feinstein's personal life. The Another Nail in the Coffin description writes that "Highspots.com's interview with Vampiro jumped to the front of line and Highspots.com hasn't looked back" since.

Smart Mark Video (SMV) entered the shoot interview market around 2000, shooting with personalities who hadn't yet done RF or Highspots shoots, such as Manny Fernandez, Dennis Carluzzo, and Sherri Martel. SMV founder and owner Mike Burns got out of the general market of shoot interview with veterans a few years later, leaving his veterans shoot interview line off on Nick Bockwinkel. He says the reason he ended on Bockwinkel is that "I felt I couldn't do a better interview or get a better person to interview without putting up a ton of money." From that point on, he decided to stick to doing shoots exclusively with indie stars for SMV's "Best on the Indies" series, new editions of which they still occasionally produce to this day.

The art & process of "shoot interviewing"

Oliver said on the May 30, 2012 In The Room podcast that "Ultimately, your product lives and dies with the entertainment value." It is this entertainment value that, as Oliver said on In Your

Head Radio in 2016, leads to "the fan votes" as a result of "their almighty dollar, and that's the only vote that matters." In fact, Oliver went so far as to say when asked in a 2017 In Your Head interview who "intimidated you the most in an interview" that "What intimidated me more than anything is the fear of no sales...not so much guests."

There are various components that make up an entertaining, and therefore successful, shoot interview. Part of the task involves picking an enjoyable guest. A lackluster interview subject is quickly evident to Hannibal, who told Hughezy Entertainment on May 21, 2020 that "You can tell they don't want to be there and they're giving like one sentence answers to all of your questions." One example he gave was Juventud Guerrera. "It was somewhere between half an hour and 45 minutes [in that] he starts tapping his foot like 'You know, hey, I'm ready to go. Finish up.' And it's like 'What the fuck, man? I paid you for an hour.'" He says that in "frustrating" situations where "I've paid them for an hour" and "they've gone through three pages of questions in 15 minutes," he makes sure to "never deal with those" interviewees again.

Another example for Hannibal of a terrible interview was "Wild" Bill Irwin (a.k.a. The Goon) on June 5, 2021. Irwin was drinking and clearly inebriated. Later that night, Hannibal described it as a "trainwreck...a torturous interview...my worst interview ever," and "the most unprofessional experience I've ever had in an interview." Not only was Irwin "very drunk," Hannibal says, but he was also "late for the interview...very defensive toward every question I asked," and "personally insulting me." Irwin was "paid for an hour long interview" that went only 17 minutes, ending with Hannibal blowing up on him for being so unprofessional.

Feinstein has cited Jimmy Snuka as probably being his worst shoot ever because Snuka wasn't at all talkative, saying on Wrestling With The Future "Everything was 'Good, brother.'...Pretty much that's all he would say about anything that I would ask him." Feinstein has also mentioned Terry Gordy as another interview like that, telling Rubber Guard Radio on March 25, 2008 that "it was like pulling teeth. We had to give him his own answers. He was kind of braindead." Gordy died weeks after that interview was conducted.

While never producing anything as outright bad as Snuka or Gordy's RF interviews, KC has had their own experiences with programs, even its trademark YouShoots, that received some disapproval for not being open enough. "It was few and far between when I wasn't able to make a connection with a talent," Oliver said on the Insiders Edge Podcast in May 2021. Often, these widely criticized YouShoot editions were of recently released WWE talents. One of those was Matt "Evan Bourne" Sydal. Another was Monster "Brodus Clay" BC, about whose edition Oliver said in a July 2020 Hughezy Entertainment interview, "I think the wildest thing he said was that he listens to his beats on the airplane. There's no debauchery. There's no anything." To a lesser degree, there was Swoggle and Teddy Long, both of which didn't get solidly bad reviews as they did mixed reviews.

In the cases of the ones that got sour reviews, many fans said the subject didn't dish enough dirt, perhaps holding out hope of being re-hired by New York. Rikishi's edition also got some negative reviews for not being adequately candid; perhaps it had to do with his sons, Jimmy and Jay Uso, being employed by WWE at the time and him not wanting to risk negatively affecting their positions. The reason for others lacking honesty are less clear, cases in point Shane Helms and Joanie "Chyna" Laurer. About the latter, Oliver said on an Insiders Edge Podcast in May 2021 "was more like an insurance seminar" than a shoot interview. Both Helms and Chyna had not recently been released from major companies at the time of the interviews, but seemed to be guarded nonetheless. Highspots also was victim to one of the "bobblehead" interviews, in their case with Dynamite Kid, so they have not been immune to the risk of doing interviews with subjects who show no personality whatsoever.

However, for those willing to show their personality, certain wrestling figures have practically made second careers out of doing shoot interviews. People like New Jack, Jim Cornette, and Raven have done so many shoots (over 15 each) that they could probably have done a shoot interview just about their memories of the various shoots they've done. Feinstein said on Rubber Guard Radio, "Raven always wanted extra paydays from us." Raven may have done the most shoot interviews of anyone, with over 25, seven alone of which were with Ring Of Honor. However, most of his shoots came in the 2000s, and since that decade, he has agreed to do many less shoots.

Others, though, are more restrictive than New Jack, Cornette, & Raven. Upon leaving major companies, certain people who may have been quality shoots like Joey Styles and Ted DiBiase Jr. stated they were available for live show bookings, but specifically mentioned that they were not willing to do shoot interviews. Meanwhile, certain pro wrestlers have released their own shoot interviews with the purpose of restricting the ability of others to market their career perspective and in the process putting all of the sales income back into their own pocket. This is the case with Rob Van Dam (The Whole F'n Shoot a.k.a. I Did It My Way, 2000), Molly Holly (Nora Greenwald: Shooting The Shi--Crap, 2005, Matt Bentley (My Perspective, 2007), and The New Age Outlaws (Oh You Didn't Know?, 2011).

Being that Oliver has produced so many successful series, he realizes that selecting a good interview subject is made all the more complex when you have multiple candidates for shows to put them on. "The way we kind of look at it is 'Which shows can this person do?' Some can only do one." He names Jim Cornette as an example of someone "who could hit all of our series":

"Cornette was a booker, so he was able to do Guest Booker. He's a lightning rod so he's able to do two editions of YouShoot. He was working creative, so he was able to do Timeline WWE and talk about all the goings on in the federation in 1997. And he was a great subject for our roasts."

Oliver said on a 2012 In Your Head podcast that "Corny knows exactly what we need, so it's very easy for me to give him the pitch on something."

In addition to a good subject who in Oliver's words on a 2017 In Your Head Interview "can have fun and...be honest,", a quality shoot interview also needs a competent interviewer. Coaxing the subject to truly open up to the camera while the red light is on is a skill that only some interviewers have. Oliver said on the Creative Control podcast that a "cogent host" must be able to "move the interview along" and at the same time "remove anyone's defenses if they're going in a little guarded."

He elaborated on a May 30, 2012 In The Room podcast that a "good interviewer" has to play two roles at once during filming: "You are not just the host, but you're the audience." They "have an internal sensor" of whether the content they are eliciting from the subject will be engaging for the prospective viewer, and if it's won't be, evoke more compelling information. On the Kayfabe Uncut (Wrestling Sauce Bottle) podcast in January 2020, Oliver equated this "ability to sit with someone and evoke" enthralling content (which he describes as stories that are "perhaps unexpected and certainly entertaining for the listener") with a "superpower," thereby implying that not all interviewers have the capability.

Feinstein discussed in his Wrestling With The Future interview the importance of a skilled interviewer:

"[Dusty Rhodes is] one of the interviews that I watch today and I don't wanna watch it because I was horrible at doing the interview. I watch a lot of interviews from the past and my interviewer skills at the beginning were atrocious. I think part of it was because I was still not a fanboy, but I was so nervous to be around some of these guys...Watching the Dusty Rhodes interview, I'm like 'Man, I should've asked him more in-depth questions' and I was not as smart to the business maybe back then as I am now. I wish I could interview probably 50% of the guys again with the knowledge that I have now of the business."

Then there comes the relationship between the two components - interviewer and interviewee. Oliver indicated on The Two Man Power Trip Of Wrestling podcast on July 5, 2016 that the best shoot interviews are generated when there is a camaraderie between the interviewer and the interviewee. He gives the example of him and Kevin Nash, saying Nash made a comment that "we've done so many of these [interviews] that he's able to kind of anticipate where everything's gonna go before I even bring it out." In that way, Oliver says, "it's kind of leading a dance and somehow sending a signal to your partner what move is coming next."

On the other hand, Oliver explained on In Your Head Radio in 2016, "you'll be able to tell the interviews where I've not met the person yet because it starts with them leaning back in their chair with their arms folded, and then eventually we're laughing together...Once they get to trust me, then things change." For those interviews that are initially challenging and require breaking through a wall, Oliver has "some tactics" that he employs, as he explained on the October 28, 2019 edition of the "It's Hughezy, Hello!" podcast: "You could always go light. You go with funny stuff....You can usually get them to laugh, and then that trust starts to come."

So, depending on the questions asked, as well as the mood of the interviewee, shoot interviews can have both positive and negative undertones, a fact which Bochicchio acknowledged in the January 2004 SLAM! Wrestling article. The bright side, he says, is that shoot interviews can be inspiring if they are "a nice tribute" that "try to stay positive and highlight [the subject's] contributions to wrestling." However, they can potentially be bleak, he explains, in that "for every positive story, there is a painful one" of "the excessive traveling [taking] a toll on their relationships with their families." Bochicchio indicates that some of the best shoots are those where the subject had a message they "wanted to get off [their] chest" at the time of filming because those are the interviews where the viewer gets "a story from [the interviewee's] heart." In this way, an interviewee having a chip on their shoulder going into a shoot interview isn't necessarily a bad thing, as it means they may have a compelling message that they want to convey to fans.

Hannibal says that pay is necessary about 90% of the time or more to get a shoot interview out of someone. The only exceptions, he says, "are unless it's a special favor or they're doing it as part of a match booking agreement." He said that Paul Roma quoted him the most ridiculous" interview fee - $2,500. He clarified in a later tweet that "that's not the most someone has ever asked but the most overpriced."

A sample payday structure was given to me by former-XPW and CZW wrestler Messiah, who told me in 2005 that he was paid $250 for his Alternative Wrestling Show (AWS) shoot interview a few years earlier. However, SMV sometimes structures pay differently for its Best on the Indies series. Burns explains: "Some got a flat fee. Others got a cut of the sales. [It] depended on what the individual wanted. No one got both...My preference was to split the sales. It felt more fair to me." Messiah, for instance, says he was paid half of the sales from his SMV release: "I don't mind telling you I made some bank on that one. HAHA."

Some wrestlers have donated their profits for their SMV Best on the Indies shoots to a charity of their choice. An example would be Jon Moxley, whose Best on the Indies was at one time when he was exploding in WWE the best-selling SmartMarkVideo DVD period: "He now donates any sales to St. Jude" Children Research Hospital, Burns said in March 2021. Rather than Burns paying the wrestlers first and then then donating, the middle man is cut out and Burns donates directly to the charity once a year: "I send it [to the charity] and then send [the wrestler] a screenshot [as proof]."

Flash in the pan ventures

KC, RF, and Highspots have been pretty much the only mainstays in the shoot interview market, and KC has stopped producing new shows in 2018. Every other company either dips in from time to time or didn't last, either because they were not serious about ingraining themselves in the market or because they got a wake-up call when their first release or first few releases didn't sell well.

One early 2000s shoot interview company was called Wrestling Universe and operated primarily out of a wrestling memorabilia store in New York City. It was in this store that many of the line's shoots were taped, with backdrops of wrestling figurines and other merchandise. The company conducted over 20 interviews with a wide range of talent. Its accomplishments include the only known extended sit-down shoots with Nicole Bass, Big Dick Dudley, Devon Storm (Crowbar), "Captain" Lou Albano, and Walter "Killer" Kowalski, as well as scooping up various former-ECW talent soon after Heyman's outfit folded for candid conversations, such as Mike Whipwreck, Nova, and Kid Kash. WU invested in registering ShootInterviews.com as their web site for a period so that people who typed that into their web browser would immediately be brought to WU products.

Wrestling Universe's shoot interview library was eventually sold to Title Match Wrestling in the 2010s, but several of the original interviews were lost and weren't inherited by Title Match in the original sale. Title Match later acquired several of the missing editions in early 2018 from a private collector. Some of the library has since gone up on TitleMatchWrestlingNetwork.com, while other editions are not for sale.

Starting around 2007, indie wrestling news web site DeclarationOfIndependents.net (DOIWrestling.net) launched the DOI Store, including shoot interviews. DOI at the time ran Women Superstars Uncensored (WSU), an all-female wrestling promotion.

They had a WSU shoot interview line, where they released shoots with indie females like Missy Hyatt, Mercedes Martinez, and Becky Bayless. There was also a general DOI shoot interview line where they released shoots with Luna Vachon, Kevin Kelly, Eddie Kingston, B-Boy, Homicide & Julius "J-Train" Smokes together, and others. DOI - both the site and the video company - stopped operating by the early 2010s.

Some short-lived companies only had a few releases. The organizers of WrestleReunion, a wrestling convention where fans could meet wrestlers, produced a few shoot interviews in the late 2000s, notably with Bruno Sammartino (hosted by Joey Styles and Bill Apter). It also had Scott Hudson-hosted editions with WCW legends Kevin Nash and Diamond Dallas Page (DDP). Similarly, Wrestle Warehouse, ran by Matt Mann, released three shoot interviews in the late 2000s. Mann was based in California, so two of his three interviews - Mike Modest and The Ballard Brothers (Shane & Shannon) - were with talent from that area, but he also did manage to score a two disc interview with Tracy Smothers. In the next decade, Off The Mark, a wrestling podcast series, delved into the shoot interview business with 2010s shoot interviews with Sabu, Drake Younger, and Ox Baker, some of which were distributed by Highspots and RF Video.

Other companies were a little more serious, releasing more than just a few shoots. Andrew Khellah ran a short-lived shoot interview production series called Pro Wrestling Diaries, with top-notch production values and aimed at hiring a few legends who had not yet done interviews with RF Video. While Pro Wrestling Diaries ran a very professionally-produced operation and gave us the only extended sit-downs with Sgt. Slaughter and Nelson Frazier (Mabel/Viscera/Big Daddy V), the company produced and released less than ten editions. Khellah later stated in a September 2014 post on Rob Feinstein's facebook wall that piracy was the reason he stopped, although he did dip his toes back into the game with a few extended YouTube interviews with talent through his new company, GO Pro Wrestling, in the late 2010s and early 2020s.

There was also a company called "No-Kayfaben" that was more serious about shoot interviews, conducting and releasing over 25 in the early and mid-2010s. The company was based out of New York and ran by Nestor Castro. Some of its interviews were posted for free on YouTube and others were sold on its web site for anywhere from $3 to $10 before shipping.

Castro wrote on the No-Kayfaben web site, "I plan on coming hard at these wrestlers! Asking the questions that I know as a fan, the people want to hear." The shoots that were posted on YouTube often were criticized by viewer comments that decried background sound, production faults, and interviewer shortcomings. While he has done many interviews, the first formal singles shoot interview that was marked as such - granted, it was only 20 minutes in duration - he has done where he wasn't paired with another wrestler that Tommy Dreamer is known to have done was with No-Kayfaben. It also did the only sit-down interviews ever with The Extreme Horsemen (Steve Corino & CW Anderson) together and Tony Mamaluke period, but in the mid-2010s, No-Kayfaben stopped releasing shoot interviews, failing to last more than a few years.

Some pro wrestling promotions, other than ROH, have also released shoot interviews. Many wrestling companies have produced one interview or only a few. For instance, One Pro Wrestling (1PW), which started producing major shows in England in 2005, launched a shoot interview line briefly, where talent it flew in from North America was interviewed on camera. Among its shoot interviews were Blue Meanie, Roderick Strong, Steve Corino, Teddy Hart and Southern Comfort (Chris Hamrick & Tracy Smothers).

Chandler Biggins and John Thorne's Absolute Intense Wrestling (AIW), meanwhile, jumped into the shoot interview game in the late 2000s, conducting interviews with The Olsen Twins (Colin Delaney & Jimmy Olsen), Masada, and Colt Cabana (as both Colt and as his alter-ego "Matt Classic"), selling the interviews through Smart Mark Video and through their own AIW web site, but they did not stay in the market long.

Germany's Westside Xtreme Wrestling (wXw) in Germany has also got involved in shoot interviews with their "Conversations" series. While they are based in Deutschland, their interviews are primarily in English. They feature mainly their own wrestlers as guests, and special attraction visitors like Chris Hero, Timothy Thatcher, and Drake Younger, but have also notably featured Shane Douglas and BJPW star Daisuke Sekimoto (in a translated interview).

DJ Hyde's Combat Zone Wrestling (CZW), which wXw has worked with extensively, also returned to the market twice in the 2010s, after a short two release venture in the mid-2000s called "Shootin' in the Combat Zone" featuring Necro Butcher and Eddie Kingston. Its first 2010s venture was called Reflections vs. Refractions and was produced by Pancoast Productions and posted three editions (one of which, the DJ Hyde one, has not been seen since it's initial release online and Hyde says it is in Pancoast's archive), releasing initially in streaming form on HybridEnt.tv and later on DVD. A few years later, it produced three more interviews under the CZW Uncut line. CZW, like AIW, stuck to producing an in-ring wrestling product in the long run.

Shoot interview marketing & delivery

RF Video originally marketed its shoots by selling them at ECW (and later indie) shows and its mall kiosks that it had in various locations throughout the East coast and Midwest. RFVideo.com launched in 1998 and allowed you to order right there on the web site with a credit card. In the early to mid 2000s, it would send seasonal newsletters via postal mail to customers, so as to update them on what was available if they didn't track new releases on the web site.

Even shoot interview product descriptions differ from company to company. RF Video has always been very gossip-oriented and always makes sure to list the juicy topics discussed, and sometimes even includes the full list of questions, although often, such as with the Johnny Kashmere 2015 shoot, only a fraction of the questions listed are asked in some cases. Kashmere is a great example of RF's casual grammatical nature in its product descriptions, as the questions list looks like it was written in Microsoft Notepad by a fifth grader. Even when advertising shoots in their postal mail newsletter, they sometimes found a way to squeeze the entire topics list into a half-page ad with small text. The duration of the interview has hardly ever been included in RF product descriptions.

Highspots, meanwhile, tends to only list a small sampling of subjects discussed in its shoot interview product descriptions, and depending on the line of shoot (i.e. traditional shoot, The Kevin Steen Show, The Interview With Alicia Atout, etc.), may or may not include run times. while KC tends to put the content descriptions in graphic form and include just keywords or a short description of topics discussed. KayfabeCommentaries.com launched in 2007, and its layout stayed the same until around the turn of 2009 to 2010 when it got a design change. It then maintained its 2010 layout for the rest of its lifespan, until it was redirected to kcvault.pivotshare.com in April 2021. This, along with its late 2019-mid 2020 "when they're gone, they're gone" DVDs sale, signaled the end of the physical DVDs era for KC. During the existence of KayfabeCommentaries.com, some product listings included run times and some didn't.

SMV often includes run times for its Best on the Indies series, but not always. The only Best on the Indies that included topics discussed was Messiah; the others are just marketed as an interview about the wrestler's career. For the non-Best on the Indies shoot interviews (i.e. Tracy Smothers, Ian Rotten, Nick Bockwinkel, etc.), run times are sometimes included and sometimes not, and a partial list of topics touched on are always listed.

Throughout the years, dating back to the early 2000s, the concept of an Internet "review" (or in some cases recap) of a shoot interview has existed. TheSmartMarks.com started doing it with some shoots shortly after the turn of the millennium, and so have other sites in more recent years such as BlogOfDoom.com and RSPWFaq.net. Those are just some of the sites that do detailed, in-depth reviews and recaps that go over most every topic discussed and recount what the personality has to say about it. There are many other sites that do much shorter, non-topic-by-topic reviews. In this way, shoot interview companies get free marketing by customers who want to share their thoughts on a shoot interview with a reader, who may then go themself purchase the interview and thereby give the shoot interview company business.

Not surprisingly, as Internet technology developed more in the mid-2000s, there was a need to move shoot interview delivery into the digital realm. The first digital on-demand venture by a major shoot interviews company was the launch of Highspots.tv in 2006. Back then, Highspots.tv featured select shoot interviews (as well as individual matches) from the Highspots library available to be purchased and watched digitally (.WMV format) in an à la carte manner. In these early days, there were also some (less than 10) short shoot interview "previews" that were free for download on Highspots.tv. When Highspots did its Ric Flair shoot in 2008, it posted the deleted scenes in this "free" digital section.

In early 2010, Highspots.tv transitioned to a subscription-based model with a fixed price per month for access to every video on the web site. It also adopted the marketing tagline "Wrestling when you want it," which it would keep for the rest of its existence. Highspots.tv would post one or more full matches or full shoot interviews per day. On a June 6, 2011 Wrestling News Live podcast, Bochicchio even offered fans who e-mailed him a two week free trial to Highspots.tv if they agreed to send him feedback about what they liked and didn't like after the two weeks had passed.

Highspots started offering some audio-only download versions of its shoots in 2013, with the first one it posted for sale (on March 27) being the 13+ hours of Ric Flair audio, but by that point, Highspots.tv was the priority for digital strategization. For instance, on February 21, 2013, Highspots.tv streamed a live shoot interview with future-husband and wife couple Mike Bennett and Maria Kanellis. Highspots.tv advertised that it would do other live shoots after Bennett and Kanellis, but never did. Bochicchio is "not sure of any benefit to doing an interview live" as it is "certainly more trouble to deal with" than taped. RF also did only two live iPPV shoots, one with Devon "Hannibal" Nicholson in March 2013 and one in September 2020 with The Nasty Boys. Asked in 2021 why live shoots are less ideal than taped ones, Bochicchio pointed out a number of reasons:

"I think live creates a lot of issues without many benefits. I don't think a live interview has the same urgency that watching a live wrestling show has for fans. We certainly haven't seen any extra viewers doing a live interview. In terms of the issues: 1. If it's not live, you can go back and ask follow-up questions that you may have missed and edit it into the appropriate spot. 2. I think on a live interview, talent is typically a little more protective. With our normal interviews, we tell talent that we can take out anything they regret later, so I think they feel safe speaking in the moment. We rarely have anyone ask us to take something out, but it does occasionally happen. 3. Generally, any mistakes can be fixed in post production, including most sound issues. 4. Live streaming, especially when...doing shoots, was very unreliable. Having a suitable upload speed wasn't necessarily available everywhere."

In 2010, SMV - which has never done a live shoot - started incorporating digital purchase availability into SmartMarkVideo.com. Its first digital release was the audio-only portion of volume 1 of the John Zandig shoot, and MP4 video-inclusive versions of some of its other Best on the Indies shoots soon followed. In 2012, Smart Mark Video launched smvod.com which allowed purchases of streaming releases, including videos of some Best on the Indies releases. Only the shoot interview portions of those releases were included, not the bonus matches parts. Burns said in 2021 that he decided to do that because only offering the matches on the DVD would "make the DVD special." RF, meanwhile, also launched its RFVideoNow.com downloads site in 2012. RFVideoNow.com provided MP4 downloads of RF releases, including its line of shoots.

However, it wasn't until a platform called "pivotshare" caught on in the wrestling community in 2015 that on demand shoot interviews really took off. With pivotshare, companies could offer fixed monthly subscription rates for all of the content on its own specific pivotshare site, but it also offered a rental option or permanent buy option for each video for those users who didn't want to buy a monthly membership.

Highspots was the first shoot interview company to launch its own pivotshare web site in 2015, with WomensWrestlingNetwork.com on September 25, for their women's wrestling releases. It used the women's site as a trial run, Bochicchio wrote in a December 16, 2015 e-mail: "We went through the steps with the WomensWrestlingNetwork.com to make sure we liked it enough to give away that much of a percentage [back to pivotshare] on the general subscription site and we feel it's worth it." The business model of pivotshare took about two fifths of all profits; however, pivotshare built a better platform than the shoot interview companies were able to build themselves, so that's why Highspots opted to use it. When Highspots decided that pivotshare was an acceptable host to use, they followed up by launching HighspotsWrestlingNetwork.com on November 24, 2015 for their general, non-female-exclusive content.

KC, RF, and Title Match Wrestling followed with their own pivotshare sites a few years later. Highspots and KC even had non-pivotshare VOD sites that either stopped being updated (in Highspots' case with Highspots.tv) or were made to redirect entirely to their pivotshare site (in KC's case with KCVault.com), and RF kept the RFVideoNow.com download site, but marketed it less after the launch of the RFVideoVault.com pivotshare site than it did before the Vault web site's creation. This evidences that Highspots, RF, and KC put their priorities more toward their pivotshare sites than their own VOD or download engines, as even though KC aired their interviews on WWNLive.com for years, they didn't fully embrace the digital transition until launching KCVault.com. SMV, on the other hand, never launched a pivotshare site.

It was around the time that Kayfabe Commentaries (mid-2018) paused in producing new content that Canadian indie wrestler Devon "Hannibal" Nicholson began becoming more visible in the shoot interview market. His YouTube channel "THE HANNIBAL TV" became serious about producing shoot interviews in the late 2010s, and by 2020, it had surpassed the combined subscribers count of Highspots, Kayfabe Commentaries, and RF Video. It makes some of its money from a Patreon account, where people who pay a nominal monthly subscription fee can watch the shoot interviews ad-free weeks before they are posted on YouTube for the general public.

Hannibal had several major coups, including the first formal sit-downs with Haku a.k.a. Meng, Sonny Onoo, Tank Abbott, David Penzer, Duke Droese, Ray Rougeau, and others. Hannibal shot with not only wrestling personalities, but also combat sports icons like Stephan Bonnar, Mark Coleman, Bas Rutten, Butterbean, and Tito Ortiz. During the coronavirus pandemic that started in 2020, Hannibal began conducting virtual shoot interviews with talent where there were split screen videos of him and the talent using webcams or other digital devices.

The rise of Kayfabe Commentaries

RF Video had some big shoot interview coups during the early to mid-2010s - Jesse Ventura, Bruce Prichard, Rey Mysterio Jr., and most notably Eric Bischoff come to mind - but by that time, most free agents who had enough of a name had already done a shoot with at least one company. This enabled Kayfabe Commentaries to gain more acclaim and rise up the ranks. Sean Oliver explained on a May 2, 2012 In The Room interview podcast how it happened, saying that the shoot interview always gave "a peak behind the magician's curtain," but "it never matured" in that they "never truly capitalized on how much fun and different this information could be disseminated."

So, as Oliver often says in interviews, KC modified shoot interviews' format. However, that wasn't all that KC improved; they also expanded production values. For instance, DVD menus (featuring chapters and trailers) were added, unlike RF Video shoots. Oliver said on the Creative Control podcast that he has seen other companies do two camera setups with no purpose; the second camera is "no tighter, it's no further out. It's like the left side of the face and then the right side of the face." KC aimed to enhance not only the content that was shot via new formats, but also to upgrade how that content was shot. In doing so, KC came up with unique programs with new themes, even marketing them by reinstating Wrestling Universe's earlier redirect of "ShootInterviews.com," this time to the KC web site. So, they never stopped promoting themself as "shoot-style programming," even while deviating from the traditional "face in a camera" format.

Both Bochicchio and Feinstein admit that Oliver's competition made them step their games up. Bochicchio says KC deserves "a lot of credit for upgrading the production of these shoots," specifically for their idea of "adding the host on camera and spending a few bucks on the lighting and the second camera...Everybody followed suit, as is the norm with this business." Similarly, Feinstein said in a Wrestling With The Future podcast that he "liked [KC's] competition because it actually made me look at my product a little bit differently and see where I need to improve."

As Kayfabe Commentaries became popular, certain memes from its programs gained steam. Likely the most famous meme in shoot interview culture is "How big is Batista's dick?" It started as a question by a fan calling himself "Sinbad" on a YouShoot edition, and took on a life of its own, getting asked by other fans on other YouShoots. Nobody with first hand knowledge knew the answer, but there have been memorable answers to the question. One was Maria Kanellis, who seemed slightly offended by the "weird" (her words) inquiry. Tony Atlas and Awesome Kong both unleashed long, hearty laughs upon hearing the question. Violent J changed the topic of the inquiry to the size of Jerry Lawler's penis. Ken Anderson changed the subject from the size of Batista's penis itself to the size of his balls and turned it into a short monologue about the condition "elephantiasis of the balls." Anderson, Sean Waltman, and Rob Van Dam all indicated that Batista's dick might not be as big as people think it is, but never gave concrete answers as to its size.

In fact, the only person to give an actual number is Iron Sheik, who said in a serious tone, "10 inch." Danny Doring, Perry Saturn, Hornswoggle, and The Honky Tonk Man also answered the comical question in astoundingly serious manners, with Doring and Scott Hall both saying they don't know the size of his dick because they've never seen him shower. In addition to the main question of whether he knew its size, dwarf Hornswoggle was also asked two variations of the question: "Are you taller than Batista's dick?" and "How tall is Torito's dick?"

Other people, such as Jim Ross and Ric Flair, have answered the question in reddit AMA ("Ask Me Anything") sessions without actually answering it directly. Ross instructed the questioner to "ASK YOUR MAMA" and Flair's response was transcribed as "How big is who? How big is WHAT?" Flair's transcriber wrote after the fact, "[Flair] was legitimately confused by the question, and then I explained to him the origins...He asked me to repeat the question several times which was just horrifying for me, then he had that reaction followed by me apologizing."

However, there have been some payoffs to this meme. For example, CM Punk claimed to know the answer in an April 19, 2017 tweet. He wrote that he wouldn't do a reddit AMA (which he has since done) "Because I know the dick size of @DaveBautista and refuse to divulge such knowledge." Batista himself responded to Punk the same day, saying "I just laughed so hard I may or may not have sharted! Not admitting anything but I'm heading to change my underwear. thanks buddy!" In the AMA that he finally did on October 17, 2019, when asked what actor or actress he wanted to work with, he wrote "Dave Batista because we're friends and we're comfortable together and I know how big his penis is!!"

Another recurring meme is "Tod is God," which originated from Sandman's YouShoot when the former-ECW champion recounted how 2 Cold Scorpio had a woman mounted and she repeatedly recited the line while being smacked across the face by his penis. Remnants of the sex story actually first surfaced in RF Video's Extreme Summit 2005 shoot with Sandman, Tod Gordon, Bill Alfonso, and Scorpio, but Sandman only talked about it for about 30 seconds and never implicated who the woman was being slapped by. The tale truly caught on from Sandman's YouShoot, due to him dramatically and animatedly telling (and demonstrating) the story from a kneeling position on the floor.

Gordon, who was the topic of the meme and line and was in the room when the story transpired, shed some light on it in his YouShoot. He claimed that the phrase actually originated from a ringside fan's sign, before the sexual encounter even happened, and revealed that the relevant woman would drive the wrestlers from town to town and that Bill Alfonso had an affair with her for a few weeks. He also claimed that several parts of the story as it had been told by others were not true. Specifically, New Jack, he said, never held a lamp over the sex act as if it was a porn scene, as Jack said he did his YouShoot edition. Gordon also claimed on his YouShoot that Sandman was not even present at the occurrence the night it happened. The "Tod is God" story would later be referenced in other KC shoots, as well as in online memes, although it did not grow as famous as how big Batistsa's member is.

Relationships between shoot interview companies

While KC has only sold its own content and SMV has only sold its own and a few indie promotions' shoot catalogs, some shoot interview companies licensed and continue to license each other's footage. For instance, RF Video sells some Highspots and KC shoot interview DVDs, but not on demand versions. Highspots and RF have done several licensing deals with each other through the years. Bochicchio says that in all cases through the years, Feinstein "approached me and said he was open to making an agreement." In the mid 2000s, after being approached by RF, Highspots gave Feinstein a list of shoots it wanted to license (basically everything RF sold at that time) and RF excluded certain ones from the deal. The other ones that weren't specifically excluded were included in the deal. Then, in 2011, Highspots did a larger licensing deal for all of the remaining RF shoot interviews that had been shot since the mid-2000s and the ones that RF had excluded from the original deal, as well as basically all of RF's other libraries, too, including ECW fancams. It also did one or two much smaller licensee deals throughout the rest of the 2010s of the new shoots RF had added to its inventory, after the initial 2006 and 2011 deals had already been made.

As a result of these deals, Highspots had permission to sell DVDs and digital versions of the RF shoots on Highspots.com and the Highspots Wrestling Network (HSWN). The DVDs part of the deal gave Highspots an advantage (then "our big calling card over RF," Bochicchio says) because its shipping times were much quicker than RF. "Rob has always been easy to work with when he needs money," Bochicchio explains. Highspots also started making some of its and RF's shoots available digitally through Vimeo and as physical DVDs through its Amazon and eBay stories. There are only a few RF shoots on Highspots' Vimeo, whereas there are many more of its DVDs at any given time on Amazon and eBay.

With the entrance of pivotshare in the mid 2010s, sharing between companies reached a new level, with shoot interview companies sharing some of their content readily with not only other shoot interview companies, but also with wrestling promotions which had their own pivotshare sites. Even then, though, KC never expanded their pivotshare site to include any RF or Highspots productions, although TitleMatchWrestlingNetwork.com did.

Bochicchio and Feinstein have a great relationship and talk to each other on a daily basis, despite being in competition for virtually the same customers. Bochicchio also mentioned his daily contact with Feinstein during the later redacted opening minute of Joey Janela's 2019 Highspots shoot.

Bochicchio and Feinstein even did a joint shoot interview at least three times (Scott Steiner, Bill Dundee, and the Hebner twins, all in the same weekend). With Steiner, Bochicchio asked most of the questions, but Feinstein got in some inquiries and towards the end, RF's Gentry even threw in three questions and one follow-up. Bochicchio asked most or all of the questions for the Hebners shoot, while Feinstein asked most or all of the questions of Dundee. "We were both watching and recording them with our own cameras at the same time," Bochicchio says. These collaborations are illustrative of the positive relationship between the two companies.

Bochicchio says that his relationship with Oliver is "exclusively business" and has been limited to exchanging some e-mails and occasionally running into each other at conventions. Bochicchio adds that Oliver "has always done good business with Highspots." Bochicchio didn't even know until being told in 2021 when being interviewed for this book that Oliver had a business partner in his KC venture - Anthony Lucignano; all of the contact between Highspots and KC has always been between Bochicchio and Oliver.

Bochicchio's company struck a deal to resell many Kayfabe Commentaries DVDs and downloads, but what was the biggest deal of all was when Highspots tweeted on November 22, 2019 that it had "come to terms on a licensing agreement w/ Kayfabe Commentaries" and would "be adding the ENTIRE LIBRARY" of KC to HSWN. In time, it did just that. Bochicchio explained how the reseller deal developed into a combined licensing and DVDs deal:

"We resold DVDs [KC] made until they stopped making DVDs. They offered to let us simply make the DVDs and give them a [report] and pay them for copies made...I generally don't like to have to do reporting on a monthly basis. It just creates more work for me and our system isn't set up like Pro Wrestling Tees where you see orders in real time. I approached them about doing a licensing deal that included DVDs and digital rights. There was a little negotiating, but I'm generally pretty fair with my offers and we came to a quick agreement."

Bochicchio mentions that because he had made "similar deals with RF Video for their library" in the past, he, when making the licensing and DVDs deal, "had an understanding of [KC's] value to us being part of the secondary market." Bochicchio said in 2021 that this KC digital "licensing deal...worked out well for both of us." Bochicchio specifies that there are no restrictions preventing KC content from being posted on Vimeo, and that KC being able to be posted on Amazon or eBay is not covered one way or another by his KC deal. However, it's definitely not worth the effort of uploading them on either of the three, he adds. He says that KC sets the prices for its DVDs that Highspots sells on Highspots.com.

As an anti-piracy consultant, I saw some of the more major shoot interview companies like Highspots, RF, KC, and SMV share limited information on piracy and customers who had been confirmed to have pirated their material. Feinstein backed up this fact that they shared information in a September 27, 2014 facebook post, writing "we are all working together and helping each other out on these matters." Part of this willingness was as a courtesy and part of it was as a convenience, having to do with them each selling each other's content.

While in modern times, shoot interview companies largely exist harmoniously, in the past, that wasn't always the case. In 2004, ROH split from RF Video due to the Rob Feinstein scandal and found itself wanting to cement itself over new rival RF as having the best shoot interviews. The feud was personal, as ROH's Sapolsky used to work with RF Video's Feinstein and Gentry at RF Video, and they each wanted to one-up one another. So, they launched their own "Straight Shootin" shoot interviews series, hosted by Gabe Sapolsky, a former-ROH employee and then-ROH booker.

The Straight Shootin line featured 44 editions in the mid 2000s, as well as eight editions of "Secrets of the Ring" (five with Raven alone), the latter of which focused on tips for wrestlers to improve themselves. The "Straight Shootin" series featured several noteworthy coups, including the only solo shoot interviews ever to this day with Mick Foley, Christian Cage, Ron Killings, Samoa Joe, and Jushin Thunder Liger. Other hits included an edition with ROH legends Samoa Joe & CM Punk together during their indie primes, as well as multiple editions with Raven & Sandman and Jim Cornette & Bobby Heenan.

There were some instances of the feud between RF Video showing itself simply in who was interviewed. In October 2004 alone, RF Video taped at least five interviews with guests who ROH also recorded shoots with. Of those five with known recording dates--RF Video back then, and still to this day, only occasionally publicized the date its interviews were shot--ROH recorded four out of the five shoots before RF did. During this era, RF Video went so far as to put a graphic before some of their shoot interviews that said "The True King Of The Shoot Interview." Similarly, on the December 2004 FUSION debut show, which was released by RF during the height of the feud between the two companies, commentary featured multiple subtle potshots to ROH by Gentry and Feinstein. In a single match on the show, Gentry called RF "the king of the shoot interview, the originators of the shoot interview" and fellow commentator Feinstein mocked the signature line of ROH commentator Gabe "Jimmy Bower" Sapolsky "Dangerousss!"

Feinstein said in an April 2020 Wrestling With The Future interview that "When I was doing Ring Of Honor, this is no secret - I was really letting RF Video go to the curb. I wasn't doing many shoot interviews. I was pretty much abusing the company that got me to the dance. I couldn't balance both." So Feinstein, by his own admission, was slacking on RF Video during the era that he was running ROH. It was during this era immediately after ROH and RF Video splitting that Feinstein became recommitted to the shoot interview game, acquiring hits like New Jack Undercover, a separate New Jack 2004 off the rails shoot, a Honky Tonk Man 2004 interview, and most notably Sabu's first on-camera interview.

Looking back on the split, Feinstein said in a January 11, 2010 Roundtable Wrestling Radio interview that "honestly, and this is a shoot, it was probably one of the best things that ever could have happened to my company as far as separating" because it allowed him "to concentrate on RF Video...To this day, RF Video is a way stronger company than it was back in 2004." Similarly, he said in a late 2004 or early 2005 DeclarationOfIndependents.net interview that he thinks RF "did more shoots in 2004 than in all of 2002 and 2003." In the same interview, he said "to tell you the truth, I liked [ROH's] Scorpio shoot a lot."

Years later in the 2010s, ROH taped roughly half a dozen more shoot interviews with its own talent, as bonus features on Best of DVDs, but the Straight Shootin era remains the only time the company seriously immersed itself in the shoot market.

The interviewee's experience

Shane Douglas, who has done shoots with Highspots, RF, ROH, Hannibal, KC, wXw, and more, admits that "Like everything in the business, shoot interviews have been perverted" and "people think that if they put the word 'shoot' on something," it will sell. He says that in 2021 "everyone wants to shoot" and a quality shoot interview has one essential component - the person "really [has] to shoot" and not sugarcoat answers. "If they ask something I don't want to answer, I can tapdance around it," but he emphasizes that that almost never happens with him: "I like to clearly enunciate everything and make it exactly clear what I'm saying."

When asked how he distinguishes an informal, free interview from a formal, paid shoot interview, he says "if someone wants to sit and record and disseminate that in some way," he generally charges. His booking manager Chris Hughes told me in 2021 that he rarely does free interviews anymore because he gets about 20 interview requests a day, some of them for sit-down shoots in front of a camera and others for podcasts, research, etc. "My manager knows what my parameters are. Typically, a shoot is going to be an hour. If it goes an hour and 15, I'm not going to say you owe me another hour," but he says if it goes two hours, there will be an additional charge: "If it goes over this time, it moves to that [price]." He adds, "I can't imagine anyone in the business being easier to work with than me" when it comes to the interview negotiation process. The shoot interview company must have common sense and basic professionalism, Douglas says. He won't do an interview "if I show up and they're shooting in some crack motel or something. I want to be safe. I want to be comfortable. I've never asked for anything other than the payoff."

Mad Man Pondo, whose shoots resume includes Highspots, SMV (twice), and Martin Cox's MatWarz a.k.a. "The Straight Talking Series," says that maybe he has been getting the short end of the stick because he doesn't always even charge when doing shoot interviews. "I've barely been paid for my shoot interviews. I think SMV is the only one who's paid me," he recalled in 2021, adding that Jake Manning "gave [him] an autographed Four Horsemen poster, which I was ecstatic about," in return for his Highspots "Fireside Chat" shoot. He explains, "I think when [a company] is doing a shoot, they're assisting [the interviewee], meaning the shoot company is helping you and getting your word out, so it's ridiculous for someone to make demands. I usually don't charge because I don't know what to charge."

Pondo doesn't like when interviewees utter "hmmm" and "ummm" filler language left and right in interviews: "One thing that aggravates me about shoot interviews is when people sit there and have to think about what they're saying." He does his "best not to do that, but even when I go back and listen to my interviews, I do do it" sometimes, "but not as bad as some people." Shoot interview companies sometimes have to reel him in. "They don't worry about whether I'm gonna go under time, but they a lot of times have to say, 'Yo, shorten your shit up a little bit' because I can go on and on and on." When he broke up with "Crazy" Mary Dobson (WWE's Sarah Logan), she was a sore subject and he was "so sensitive" about her that he would have to tell interview outlets that he didn't want to be asked about her.

Chris Hamrick, who has done shoots with Highspots, 1PW, Bert Duckwell, and FWA, somewhat echoes what Pondo said about repetitive language in shoots. He says that there are many shoots where people "say the same things over and over," and being that he realizes that "there's only so many things you can say" in a shoot interview, he likes when people spice up their answers and include fresh takes on common topics. He believes that shoots have evolved in that at one time, they were often a burial of people who the interviewee didn't like, and nowadays, they've become more like a back-and-forth, friendly talk. "When I watch a shoot, I don't want to watch someone down someone," Hamrick explains. "I'm more interested in what they've been through and where they want to go." He says that often, a shoot interview company will ask if there's any topic that's off limits, and he always says that any topic is fair game, and adds that he doesn't really set a time limit for shoots: "We go until we don't feel like going anymore."

Like Douglas, Hamrick emphasizes that he only ever asks for the payoff, and like Pondo, he doesn't agree with people who ask for this and that amenity in return for an interview. "If it's not in front of a camera, it's free," he explains, although there are exceptions, as, like Pondo, he also hasn't even charged for all of his formal shoots, such as FWA. His 1PW shoot with Smothers happened very spontaneously, he adds, as he and his Southern Comfort partner were just in the locker room shooting the breeze and decided to make a video out of it. He says that the thing about the dual shoot with Smothers as compared to a solo shoot is that he consciously couldn't talk over the talkative Smothers. That being said, he admits that if anyone is going to have the spotlight over him on any part of an interview, it should be Smothers, who worked "10 times as many places as" he did.

Konnan, who has done shoots with Highspots, RF, ROH, and Hannibal, says that in order to be able to offer engaging stories in his shoots, "I never get questions ahead of time. I like to be surprised and react accordingly." He emphasizes that "I was doing shoot interviews before they were fashionable for Wade Keller's Torch Talk" and that he knew, even "early on, [that] everybody just works the fans, even on interviews." His approach, he explains, tends to be different: "I'd rather just tell the truth, which is what I always did. A lot of times, my opinion gets heat because nobody wants to be criticized or read anything bad about themselves." Konnan told me that that he generally doesn't hold back when doing shoots, except when it comes to sex stories: "There is no topic that is off limits [with me], but if ...they are married, I'm not gonna bury that person with infidelity shit."

Konnan says of the process of negotiation going into a shoot interview between a company and an interviewee: "I'm easy with that. [I ask and say] 'How long is it? You can ask what you want...That's my price." Another reason he's going to make sure he gets something worthwhile out of a shoot is that "I don't particularly like talking about myself all the time. I get tired of talking about wrestling," so "I don't say this to be presumptuous, but if I'm traveling and I'm gonna sit for two hours plus, it's gonna cost."

"Pitbull" Gary Wolf, who has done shoots with RF and - during the coronavirus webcam remote era - Hannibal, as well as three "Legends Of Extreme" panel shoots for Highspots, says that a worthwhile shoot interview needs "a great person asking the questions," and the questions have to be about "topics that have a lot of controversy" associated with them. Wolf always has the freedom to answer questions how he wants, as he's "never been told [by a shoot interview company] how to answer a question." He also doesn't like questions being shared with him in advance: "I'd rather you not tell me [the questions ahead of time] and then just throw [them] to me during the course of the interview." When someone wants to give him the questions ahead of time, "that shows me the interview guy is nervous and doesn't want to say the wrong thing or is afraid to piss me off."

For these reasons, he categorizes himself as someone who blossoms with the right interviewer - "to get info out of me, you gotta ask me the right questions. A lot of people want to get controversy from me," and they will get that if they ask questions strategically. Only some interviewers pass this test, he finds - "I think sometimes they're kind of nervous and they kind of beat around the question they're trying to ask." If the interviewer is straightforward with their questions, "then I'll tell you the truth," he says. "If this is a shoot, shoot it and tell me what's up. You may not like the answer, but I'll answer it." After all, the fans, he says, will be the ones to benefit from hearing the behind-the-scenes stories.

The exception, he specifies, like Konnan does, is sex stories. "People have families. Some of these guys are married now," Wolf explains. "That's being respectful. If it's something that will affect a family member or someone's partner, I wouldn't go there." Another part of being polite, he mentions, comes into play in Q&A sessions and panel shoots with multiple people, as opposed to a solo shoot. He has the "pure courtesy" to "let [someone] finish before I'm gonna say anything else. If you're gonna interrupt me, then I might as well put my first down your fucking throat so you can't talk." He enjoys doing Q&A sessions because "someone will remember something" remarkable and it will spur more stories in the memories of the other participants: "You get more stories that way."

Wolf is willing to do unpaid shoots depending on the situation, but says that he is only going to give some of the juiciness ("a little bit of the scoop"), whereas if he's getting paid, he will not hide anything. Before covid, shoot interview pay was consistent, he explains, but during covid, interviewing companies are generally willing to pay more because times are tough with less shows. He says that "every year, the expectations change" for the product that an interviewee will deliver, since "someone is more over than someone else,"and someone different has recently been released from WWE, thereby making them a popular conversation topic among fans.

Alternatives to the traditional shoot interview (Wrestling personalities-hosted shows/Shoot interviews with live audiences) (1,848)

There are ways of varying the format of a shoot interview in its traditional form, to avoid just having a wrestler in front of the camera and an interviewer behind it. One method, which became popular in the mid-2010s, involved the host of the interview, a wrestling personality as opposed to a shoot interview company director, sitting on camera with the guest(s) and shooting along with them. Kevin Steen, at his peak on the indies in 2013 and 2014, hosted a series of this sort, The Kevin Steen Show, for Highspots. "We picked Steen because he was the leader of the independent wrestling pack and he could get anybody he wanted to appear on the show," Bochicchio explains. Steen would have a special guest (or two guests, if a tag team) on each show and interview them about their career. The Kevin Steen Show released 22 DVDs and 23 editions total - Jimmy Jacobs and Truth Martini's interviews were released on the same DVD, but as separate on demand videos. Steen was by far the most popular Highspots hosted series, but there were others during that era, like Steve Corino's Old School and Dr. Tom Prichard's Wanted Dead Or Alive.

When Steen left for WWE in 2014, Highspots recruited The Best Friends (Trent Barretta & Chuck Taylor) to take his spot. "Chuck and Trent were actually suggested by Kevin to 'replace him,'" Bochicchio said in 2021. "We didn't see the potential. That is all credit to Kevin. I think he saw that these guys were the leaders of the after party and would make interesting hosts." Chuck and Trent had a long run with a self-titled show, which focused often on fewer wrestling topics than toilet humor-type topics unrelated to wrestling. Best Friends ran until 2019, when they closed their show with two appropriate guests: Jerry Lynn, who they had consistently asked their other guests for their best story about, and Mikey Whipwreck, Trent's trainer.

During the rise of Best Friends, Highspots also used many other wrestling personalities to run "hosted shows," among them Rob Naylor (Hitting The Highspots), Rockstar Spud a.k.a. Drake Maverick (I'm With Spud), and Excalibur and Dan Barry together (A Gentleman and a Scholar), but Best Friends remained the most successful during that period. It was during this period - the late 2010s - that the wrestling personality-hosted program peaked, with new releases being constantly put out. When asked what characteristics its many hosts had in common to make them candidates for the job, Bochicchio interestingly responded that it wasn't about the attributes they shared, but rather what was important was the qualities that made each person unique: "I'm not sure any of them have something in common, but we pick people for a variety of reasons as a host."

For instance, for Spud it was "his knowledge and professionalism" that got him the gig. The knowledge came in that Highspots "wanted somebody, at the time, that could basically interview the entire Impact roster and he fit the bill," and that credibility due to his involvement on-screen with Impact Wrestling. His professionalism, Bochicchio explains, is evident in the fact that "if Spud says he'll be ready to go at 2 pm, he'll be ready and there won't be any excuses." This could be contrasted to Corino, Bochicchio says, who was "generally unreliable" in that "he just wouldn't commit to anything in advance" and "the last time we 'worked together' [on an Old School episode], he double-booked himself." Bochicchio says that "we really wanted to do more with" Corino in the shoots realm, but it didn't work out that way.

Another way to spice up a shoot interview is to have a wrestler or even a panel of wrestlers shoot in front of a live crowd. It had been done dating back to the early '90s with John Arezzi's Weekend of Champions conventions. ECW picked it up on a more public platform in the mid-90s during the company's annual "CyberSlam" weekend. ECW would then sell the Q&A on VHS through RF Video. There are a few ways of doing this - one with the audience asking the questions (a question and answer, or Q&A, session), one with an interviewer asking all of the questions and the only audience interaction being cheers, boos, and laughs, and a third way with both methods combined.

1PW and Ian Rotten's IWA Mid-South used Q&As to sell as video tapes and DVDs and thereby collect additional revenue from non-wrestling footage shot during some of their more star-studded weekends. 1PW also hosted, taped, and sold Q&As with amalgamations of stars together, as well as individual ones with Ric Flair, Bret Hart, The Iron Sheik, and Rob Van Dam, among others. Meanwhile, IWA Mid-South did them twice per year in the mid-2000s during their annual King of the Death Match and Ted Petty Invitational (TPI) weekends, distributing them through SMV. In the mid-2000s, Highspots also shot and released a whole bunch of Q&A sessions at various fanfests that were within driving distance of its North Carolina headquarters.

Q&As exploded during the 2010s. For instance, RF Video used a Philadelphia Dave & Buster's to host its fan-attended Eric Bischoff vs. Bruce Prichard Debate moderated by Chris Jericho in 2015. The event took place the afternoon of the Royal Rumble a few blocks away, and Jericho came to Feinstein with the idea of moderating the debate, not the other way around. Feinstein said on a January 2015 Creative Control podcast that Prichard told him that he and Bischoff's desire to do the debate came from nights of drinking and consequent butting of heads with each other about the Monday Night Wars. It was later released on DVD and streaming platforms.

As live streaming technology became more advanced, it allowed for live broadcasts of Q&A sessions. Highspots live-streamed panels at WrestleCon in 2016, and it was done on a larger scale with StarrCast, a convention headed by Conrad Thompson. The business model of StarrCast was based in part on live-streaming Q&As through FITE TV. Some of the panels were simple Q&A sessions, while others were live-taped versions of already existent podcasts. StarrCast allowed you to buy each panel session individually on demand, or to buy them all together at a group rate.

The 2018 StarrCast occurred in conjunction with Cody Rhodes and The Young Bucks' "All In" supershow and the 2019 version occurred as a partnership with the launch of AEW. StarrCast had some impressive coups, such as solo sessions with Jon Moxley fresh out of WWE, as well as CM Punk, Insane Clown Posse, Sting, Mick Foley, and Bret Hart. Furthermore, Undertaker and Ric Flair were announced and then cancelled for StarrCast Q&A sessions at various points, too.

Not all shoot interviews include video footage; some are just audio, and may be part of a weekly or regularly recurring schedule of a particular person or brand. These are often termed "podcasts." For instance, Dave Meltzer used to host "Wrestling Observer Live" on Eyada.com, an early Internet radio talk show network that lasted less than two years, from 1999 to 2001. Wrestling Observer Live started in October 1999 and it continues under a different name to this day. On it, Meltzer conducts non-kayfabe interviews with wrestling personalities all the way up to Ric Flair and even then-WWE stars during that turn of the millennium era of the show.

The then-upstart XPW also jumped on the podcasts bandwagon in 1999, as its webmaster Tony T. would conduct out-of-character audio interviews with XPW personalities in .ram (RealPlayer) format, called "XPW Radio." For instance, back in 1999, his interview with then-XPW talent Nicole Bass was posted on XPWrestling.com and featured Bass emotionally telling all about her sexual harassment lawsuit against WWE, which was the talk of the wrestling community at the time.

Podcasts continued for the next decade during the 2000s, but they didn't boom and go mainstream until the 2010s. Sean Oliver said on the GeniusCast with Lanny Poffo on October 15, 2019 that he thinks his company deserves some credit for "what's become this wrestling podcast boom." However, the wrestling podcast rise also has had an effect on his business - a negative effect, that is. As wrestlers share their stories and fans can listen to them on podcasts without paying for it, the demand for interviews which fans are willing to pay for has not surprisingly decreased, also.

In this respect, it makes sense that Oliver told PWMania.com in February 2015 that a wrestling personality's "legacy is what should now be making them money," especially "if they are out of the ring." Not only can it make them money, but it should make them money, Oliver says - "they deserve to make a living off of" that legacy instead of "giving away their story for free." KC, he argues, fulfills the compensation side of the bargain in that "we pay and pay fairly to record and sell a part of that creator's legacy." However, he points out that KC's job is made harder when that creator (the subject of the interview) does "a shoot interview for free for two hours on a podcast" because it prostitutes the subject's story and thereby lessens the value of their subsequent paying interviews.

He went so far as to say on In Your Head Radio in 2016 a wrestler prostituting themself on a podcast is "going to devalue the particular legend or the particular talent that's on the show in the marketplace." So, in the process of the market for interviews that fans will pay for dropping, so too has the amount of money some of the more regularly podcasting wrestling personalities can ask for on the progressively rarer occasion that they do opt to do a for-pay shoot interview.

Even so, Oliver has implied that podcasts will never accomplish the same magic as an in-person video shoot. "I don't think you can necessarily compare the podcast with a well-produced shoot interview...That energy and that trust is something that floats in the air and it doesn't go through these wires here so easily," Oliver said on the Insiders Edge Podcast.

Other times, putting forth an alternative shoot interview simply involves a shoot company releasing an interview with someone who did not accomplish most (or even any) of their fame in wrestling. RF Video has done it with actor Corey Feldman and baseball player Lenny Dykstra, KC interviewed Insane Clown Posse (ICP), and No Kayfaben shot with famed rapper Cuban Link. Matt Striker hosted the Feldman shoot, while Tommy Dreamer anchored Dykstra's interview.

Oliver said on Inside The Ropes in December 2013 that even though ICP had wrestling experience, one of the motivations for interviewing them was that "there's a cross-over opportunity from a business standpoint" wherein fans of their music may buy the program. In fact, when I was working for KC as an anti-piracy consultant, Oliver e-mailed me the night before the ICP YouShoot's release and told me to be on the lookout for it being illegally posted on music forums and not just the usual wrestling sites, and he was right about that prediction.

Bootlegging & Piracy

Feinstein brought up bootlegging as early as March 10, 1997 with an RSPW post titled "RF Video warns tape dealers selling ECW and More" that read, in part:

"RF video is also going to take legal action against anyone selling our shoot interviews especially the New Jack- Bill Alfonso-Tommy Rich and more...We will purchase tapes under a secret identity from dealers and if you sell them we will have to face legal action."

During the early days of RF shoots, at the end of the interview, the host would sometimes tackle the bootlegging issue in comical fashion by making jokes on tape about what they would have done to people who bootlegged the tape. For instance, when asked what would happen to bootleggers, New Jack said on his 1996 interview:

"If you all sell this tape and don't give me a cut of my shit, I'm 'a fuck you up. Straight up...I'm serious. [stands up and puts his face close to the camera] I want my money. I'm not bullshitting. Ain't that right, Rob? I want my fucking money."

Meanwhile, on the Tommy Rich interview, Rich said "We gonna sue them" and Feinstein followed up with "We're gonna kill them," which he also said at the end of the first Justin Credible shoot. Taz, too, said on his edition that "I will fucking kill you" bootleggers, and added what sounded like a half sarcastic elaboration - "Don't be an asshole and go and make money. Let Rob and RF Video make all the money." During the last five seconds of the interview, Taz asked if RF has "a lot of bootleggers" and Eric Gargiulo responded that they did, "especially with our shoot interviews."

Feinstein said on the Balls Mahoney shoot that he's "gonna sue" bootleggers and "sick you [Balls] on them," to which Balls elaborated "Chairshots all around." Balls' tag team partner, Axl, said "I'm gonna fucking beat [bootleggers] to death" on his edition. Feinstein's warning on teh first Sandman shoot was that "Sandman's gonna cane you" bootleggers, and, it was Taz who Feinstein said he would sick on bootleggers on the Bill Alfonso shoot. Alfonso added, "We're not trying to get rich here, but we're just trying to make everybody happy and keep doing this, and bootleggers have been around for years and years."

Highspots owner Michael Bochicchio, meanwhile, has faced bootlegging and piracy since the mid-2000s. He says "My business is primarily focused on creating content. After creating it, the only thing I expect is the ability to control its distribution." He equates piracy to theft, saying "The most frustrating thing as a creator is seeing your hard work posted by some anonymous user for everybody to pillage...When the footage is pirated, it's the equivalent of somebody breaking into your home, taking your new television and the police can't/won't do anything about it." He says that the next logical step is to take an approach to fight piracy: "If you are a content creator, what is the point of your hard efforts if you're not going to protect your own work? You wouldn't leave the front door of your house wide open for anybody to take what is inside. Why do the same for your content?"

Highspots temporarily used an approach during the late 2000s or early 2010s where they would require a certain amount (generally 250) of pre-orders for a shoot interview before they would start shipping them. This assured that they would get back the money that they had put in to create the production and reduce the money they would lose on a given DVD to piracy. The approach only was largely temporary, and Highspots soon went back mostly to just releasing shoot interviews as their production of each interview was completed.

Another, more effective and practical way of combating piracy that shoot interview companies have used is to hire an anti-piracy consultant. Kayfabe Commentaries co-founder and co-owner Sean Oliver says "Piracy is a stark reality for serious content producers, and much like an exterminator, there comes a time when producers must call upon someone to handle that unfortunate reality." That is where my own experience comes into play. At some point or another, I have worked for all three major shoot interview companies of the 2010s era - Highspots, Kayfabe Commentaries, and RF Video, as well as Smart Mark Video, who has a "Best on the Indies" series. There was even a short period where I worked for all four of those companies at once. My job was to, in return for a monthly fee, go around dark corners of the Internet to piracy sites and video sharing sites and send copyright infringement notices to the web hosts of the files in order to disable them, thereby maximizing return on shoot interview profits.

While Highspots and Kayfabe Commentaries have taken serious precautions against piracy for a number of years, RF Video's approach has been more sporadic. By vetting customers, there was a period from 2014 to 2016 where RF was doing a fantastic job of preventing their new releases from being leaked to Xtreme Wrestling Torrents (XWT), which is where many new releases originate from to this day. One specific instance of a customer getting caught pirating shoot interviews that they purchased was in September 2014, when a customer made the mistake of using their real name as their user name to leak the then-new Eric Bischoff RF Video shoot interview on XWT. Feinstein made a facebook post on September 27 that he and the customer "settled for a small $1000 penalty and a promise he would never do it again." However, starting in about 2016, RF appeared to, at least outwardly, not actively be fighting piracy, as its full shoots on YouTube would not be pulled like they once were.

There have been some instances of RF Video and Highspots giving non-employees permission to post its shoot interviews in full or almost in full on YouTube. Rick Martel's handlers obtained permission from RF Video to post his full shoot interview on YouTube in a video that has been public on YouTube since April 7, 2013. There is no word on whether Martel's brand paid RF to do this. Then, starting in February 2017, a YouTube channel called "WCWFanForever" started posting - with authorization from RF Video - full shoot interviews or extended parts of them that focused on the wrestler's WCW tenure. Feinstein, asked about this, says "he paid us a lot of money for that." Highspots also authorized a 20 minute Lex Luger segment from its own shoot interview library to be posted on the WCWFanForever channel, likely in return for payment, too.

One embarrassing moment for an interviewee came when Stevie Richards mentioned to interviewer Feinstein that he had watched RF's Jesse Ventura shoot and starts talking about Jesse's fight for wrestling unionization before Feinstein interrupts and asks "Did I give you a copy?" Richards, knowing he's been caught, raises his eyebrows and admits that he downloaded the audio from DropBox. He jokes that Feinstein can "deduct "half" of his pay for the shoot interview he's doing at the moment (since it was audio only), although Feinstein has a sense of humor during the whole discussion, which lasts less than a half minute in total.

END OF BOOK

Special thank you to my late friend Jonathan Barber for working on a very well put together retrospective on the Xtreme Pro Wrestling (XPW) organization as well as an in depth story on the advent of shoot interviews in professional wrestling. I would like to take this time to thank him for giving me the blessing to release his works for you the readers & those he loved working with. He was a kind and intelligent individual who I had the pleasure of interacting with over the years. I would also like to thank his mother Joyce, and my friend Seth for supporting me with all of this. God bless you all and Thank You. Go to www.thexpwwrestling.com for more information on XPW.

- *Conrad C.*

(Photos taken at Beautiful Disaster by my good friend, thank you brother!)

Made in the USA
Las Vegas, NV
03 January 2024

83879642R00108